Advance P

"David Bernstein has written an important book which deserves to be read widely and be thoroughly discussed in our community. This book is a powerful defense of liberal values.... Bernstein's treatment is nuanced and respectful, showing understanding for the goals even as he critiques the methods of woke culture and shows us cases where it leads to antisemitism."

—Rabbi Yitz Greenberg, American scholar, author, and rabbi

"David Bernstein had spent his career on the left and involved in mainstream Jewish organizations. His timely and important book recognizes the anti-liberal tendencies now dominant on the progressive left and the threats those tendencies posed to America and to the Jewish community. He resisted moving in this direction for a long time, but current circumstances warrant his conversion. As the great John McClane has said, 'Welcome to the party, pal.'"

—Tevi Troy, Presidential historian and former White House aide, author of *Fight House: Rivalries in the White House from Truman to Trump*

"In every age, hatred of Jews cloaks itself in different moral garb. Today's fashion goes by many names, Wokeism, Social Justice, Critical Social Justice, etc., but the historical commonalities are unmistakable—as are its ineluctable prescriptions. In clear, plainspoken language, David Bernstein denudes the profoundly unsettling relationship between woke ideology and antisemitism. This is an urgent message few people want to hear, but one that everyone needs to understand."

—Peter Boghossian, author and philosopher

"A provocative and reasoned warning about the rise of antisemitism and the precious legacy of classical liberalism."

—Rabbi David Wolpe, Max Webb
Senior Rabbi, Sinai Temple

"Straining to find common cause with the Woke is a recipe for self-destruction for American Jews. Bernstein's valiant and essential call to awaken us to this truth comes not a moment too soon."

—Abigail Shrier, author of *Irreversible Damage*

"Like moths attracted to the flames that can consume them, Jews have long sought salvation in ideologies that ultimately sought to destroy them. It happened with communism and is being repeated with young Jews' visceral embrace of 'wokeness' that in the name of freedom and equality, snuffs out freedom of thought and equality for Jews. David Bernstein's thoughtful and alarming account of precisely why and how 'woke' ideology threatens the Jewish people could not come at a more critical moment. One can only pray that those who most need to read this book do so before it is too late."

—Daniel Gordis

"Even if you, as a progressive like me, end up thinking that David overstates his case in *Woke Antisemitism*, the book, especially if read with a wider lens, is an invaluable examination of the role dogma plays in our society, and more particularly how Jewish groups navigate it. Dogmas that teach there's something noble in persecuting political opponents because we're 'obviously right' are not only reminiscent of McCarthyism, but also feed binary (and conspiratorial) thinking, creating fertile ground for one of the most persistent conspiracy theories—antisemitism—to grow."

—Kenneth S. Stern, director Bard Center for the Study of Hate and author most recently of *The Conflict over The Conflict: The Israel/Palestine Campus Debate*

"After decades of faithful service to the Jewish community, David Bernstein has taken on the fight of his life: to resist the debilitating impact of wokism and help the Jewish community remain faithful to Jewish values and interests. Compellingly written and powerfully argued, this book is an essential contribution to a long-overdue debate."

—Yossi Klein Halevi, senior fellow, Shalom Hartman Institute

"In his trenchant study of woke antisemitism, David Bernstein exposes the perils of this latest iteration of the socialism of fools."

—James Kirchick, columnist, *Tablet*

"David Bernstein has written a bold and important book, filled with in-depth research and personal experiences. David spent years leading important liberal organizations. His book resonates with intelligence and profound observations. A must read for anyone who wants to understand trends in 21st century liberalism."

—Rabbi Ammiel Hirsch, Senior Rabbi, Stephen Wise Free Synagogue

"David Bernstein, son of an immigrant, grew up learning by arguing. In his righteous, yet poignant, book he shows how Jewish institutions have surrendered to woke ideology, leading them to forget the rationale behind the value of debate and to lose the passion for it. *Woke Antisemitism* is an urgent and eloquent plea to retake and preserve Jewish reverence for both deep wisdom and pragmatic problem-solving. If the Jewish community can succeed in doing so, it will be an inspiration to other groups seeking liberation from ideological oppression."

—Sally Satel, M.D., senior fellow, American Enterprise Institute and Lecturer, Yale School of Medicine

"An urgent, painful, and refreshingly self-critical examination of woke antisemitism and its impact on American Jewish life today. Replete with illuminating anecdotes, Bernstein's courageous call for a re-centering of Jewish communal relations and advocacy deserves the widest possible hearing."

—Jonathan D. Sarna, University Professor and Joseph H. & Belle R. Braun Professor of American Jewish history, Brandeis University

"Antisemitism has long been one of the most pervasive and troubling of mankind's many forms of fratricide, in large part because of its flexibility. American conservatism had a historical problem with Jew-hatred—but so did Islamism, the Catholic Church, and the Communist Soviet Union. And now, in *Woke Antisemitism*, David Bernstein argues that some of the worst anti-Semites of today can be found on the 'woke' left. His case is persuasive: any movement that treats disproportionate success as de facto evidence of the oppression of others will be hard on a high-performing minority, and any that sees 'Zionism as racism' will predictably clash with the Jewish community on key issues.

As a conservative Black man—a member of another group often targeted by these same 'activists'—I agree with Bernstein that Jews seeking to avoid bigots should look all around rather than simply to their right, and I strongly recommend his book."

—Wilfred Reilly, author of *Hate Crime Hoax*, Assistant Professor of Political Science at Kentucky State University

"Wokism is an illiberal ideology that pretends to be humane and progressive. In places where it thrives—universities, newsrooms, cultural institutions—it breeds rancor, bullying, silencing, canceling, and even antisemitism. As David Bernstein shows in this deeply-researched and cogently-argued book, many Jewish organizations, including schools and synagogues, have unwittingly embraced this misguided and often Jewish-averse philosophy. Bernstein's account is full of disturbing examples but also rich with solutions to the growing problem of 'woke antisemitism.' Required reading for anyone concerned about the well-being of American Jewry."

—Christina Hoff Sommers, philosopher and author of *Who Stole Feminism?* and *The War Against Boys*

"There is a new ascendant politics on the Left which holds that the world is divisible into oppressed and oppressor groups, that America was founded as a slaveocracy and persists in its pervasive abuses against minority groups six decades after the end of Jim Crow, the emergence of the civil rights and welfare states, and the continuous practice of affirmative action, and that the world is an ongoing struggle between righteous indigenous peoples and violent settler colonialists that justifies policies of reparation and transfer from oppressor to oppressed based on those enacted in post-apartheid South Africa. Is this ideology good for the Jews? Is it good for American democracy? David Bernstein has been a witness to the emergence, incubation, and rise to power of this ideology, which has gone by various names over the decades, but has always regarded successful minority groups as especially problematic, and maintained an open animosity toward the Jewish state in particular, recently obtained new purchase within American progressivism and the organized Jewish community itself amidst the ideological enthusiasms of recent years. His new book brings to bear his long experience and familiarity contending with this ideology and makes a strong and forthright case that it is indeed bad for the Jews and American democracy."

—Wesley Yang, American essayist, columnist for *Tablet* magazine

"David Bernstein did not want to write this book. He came to his critique of both the American left in which he has spent his life and the Jewish institutions to which he has devoted that life grudgingly and slowly, but therefore also thoughtfully and with the highest regard for the aims those institutions mean to serve. That makes for a powerful, compelling, and alarming case that anyone concerned for the future of American Judaism must read."

—Yuval Levin, senior fellow, American Enterprise Institute, and author of *A Time to Build*

"David Bernstein has given us an important and timely book on the 'woke' ideology of the far left and the dangers it poses both to liberal values and to the Jewish community.

Drawing on a wide range of sources and his decades-long experience as a senior community leader, David traces the evolution of 'wokeness' from its roots in postmodern and postcolonial thought, through the disgraceful Durban Conference of 2001, to its most pernicious manifestations today. And in showing how antisemitism is an inevitable component of the ideology, he touches on its most central and consequential concepts—'whiteness' and racism, oppression and intersectionality, privilege and equity, critical race theory and 'liberated' ethnic studies, political correctness and cancel culture. He also provides detailed accounts of how Jewish organizations and schools have advanced the very ideological paradigms that put Jews and Israel in the crosshairs.

Policymakers, scholars, and lay readers alike will benefit from this rich and invaluable treatment of a deeply important subject. And we all should heed David's demand that we return critical thinking and the uncensored exchange of ideas to our public discourse. This book is essential reading!"

—Elan S. Carr, Former United States Special Envoy to Monitor and Combat Anti-Semitism

WOKE ANTISEMITISM

How a Progressive Ideology Harms Jews

DAVID L. BERNSTEIN

A WICKED SON BOOK
An Imprint of Post Hill Press
ISBN: 978-1-63758-767-6
ISBN (eBook): 978-1-63758-768-3

Woke Antisemitism:
How a Progressive Ideology Harms Jews

Cover Design by Matt Margolis

Post Hill Press
New York • Nashville
WickedSonBooks.com

Published in the United States of America
1 2 3 4 5 6 7 8 9 10

For all the "thought criminals" and courageous people,
Jewish and non-Jewish alike, whose consciences will not
allow them to go along with a totalizing ideology.

CONTENTS

FOREWORD

BY NATAN SHARANSKY

August 2022

Like many Jews from the Former Soviet Union, both in the U.S. and in Israel, I am concerned. I am concerned about the ideological environment in the U.S., a global superpower, a beacon of hope for all of humanity and the main defender of freedom and human rights in the world. I am concerned about the emergence of a dogma—some call it "woke" ideology—not unlike the totalizing ideology I grew up with in the Soviet Union, which has taken the American left by storm and with it many American cultural institutions. I am concerned that many of my good friends in the American Jewish community who for all the right reasons want to be part of the human rights and social justice movements of their time, do not fully recognize the danger of this ideology, both in how it will impact the US and how it will influence attitudes toward Jews and Israel.

Growing up in the Soviet Union, there was an ideology that we had to learn in grade school and in the university and were forced to repeat at every opportunity. This ideology stated that the entire history of the world is a fight between the privileged and unprivileged, between those who have and those who have not. The ideology held that people of good will must join in a fight by the proletariat against the capitalists. And the proletariat are always right because they are the victims. The ideology held that capitalists should be deprived of their right to speak because when they speak they merely justify thousands of years of exploitation. That very ideology was used as a pretext to kill tens of millions of people for belonging to the "wrong" class, to the "wrong" nation, or to the "wrong" political views, dissidents and non-dissidents alike, many Jews among them.

In the beginning, many Jews, inspired by the progressive dream about the world of equals, joined the revolution. In the end this ideology was weaponized specifically against Jews.

For Soviet Jews, the connection between antisemitism and anti-Zionism could not have been clearer. We knew that both the anti-cosmopolitan and anti-Zionist campaigns were aimed at Jews. Whenever Jews were scapegoated, the Soviets raised the volume of the rhetoric against Israel, which often carried full-fledged blood libel of "Zionists" operating under cover and the ever-present Rothschild family, who supposedly controlled the American media and other institutions. Soviet rhetoric constantly went after its "agent of America," the Zionist, imperialist state of Israel.

With the collapse of the Soviet Union and the triumph of Western, liberal values in the 1990s, I became convinced that this hateful, antisemitic ideology had been defeated once and for all and that there was no place in the liberal order for such radical dogma. We fought against it and defeated it. Unfortunately, now we see it has come back in new forms, often in the name of social justice. In woke ideology, if you substitute the word race for class, you will get almost the exact same Marxist-Leninist dogma in which we were indoctrinated in schools that became the basis of the hatred against dissidents and anyone who dared question the party line.

In today's ideological movements, I see some of the same forces that I experienced in the Soviet Union—forces that demonize the Jewish state—and an expectation, sometimes implicit and sometimes explicit, that Jews give up aspects of their identities in order to conform to these ideological whims. Jews should be able to live in the fullness of their Jewish identity and not be forced to rid themselves of the "undesirable" aspects, such as their relationship to Israel. Going along with progressive dictates is not nearly as cost-free as many Jews might imagine.

I grew up in a place where the authorities proclaimed: "the proletariat of the world unite." In today's conception of intersectionality, haters of Jews unite. In the Soviet Union, there were good nations and bad nations—good nations were part of the struggle against the global capitalists and bad nations were opposed to it. In woke ideology, there are good identities and bad identities. In this worldview, the most victimized identity is Palestinian and the worst identity is Israeli, that which represents the last colonial project. Intersectionality unites woke progressive theory with the most primitive forms of antisemitism.

Many on the woke left diminish the Holocaust, calling it "white on white crime," and declaring that such crimes are unimportant in the grand sweep of history in the struggle between oppressed and oppressors. When asked why she didn't mention antisemitism, one diversity trainer at Yale Law School responded that she covered antisemitism by discussing anti-black racism, as some Jews are black. She didn't recognize there could be antisemitism against people who are not black. Repeated often enough, such absurdities become part of a supposedly noble fight for equality. It's not at all surprising that in today's ideological environment, antisemitism is downgraded and swept under the rug. The Jew, at once successful and oppressed, only complicates this simplistic ideological picture.

David Bernstein has written an important book on how an ideology that has taken hold in America functions to spread antisemitism. He argues that the very fixed concept of privilege—white privilege, male privilege, etc., which defines precisely who is the oppressor and who is the oppressed by virtue of their identity, will inevitably lead to the Jewish community and Israel being labeled the oppressor. Indeed, any ideology that connects identity to power will ultimately be used to assert Jewish power over the lives of the oppressed. It's already happening.

Bernstein also offers a roadmap for extricating the Jewish community and, by extension, American society, from this woke dystopia. He argues that American Jews should build a new set of allies, particularly among immigrant communities who love America and want it to live up to its democratic ideals. He lays out a very specific plan for how American Jews can prevail. While I will leave it to others to decide with whom American Jews should partner, I know from experience that no true ally would advance a racist ideology that puts Jews and other minorities in harm's way. I urge my friends in the Jewish community to give Bernstein's ideas careful consideration.

One of the greatest moments for American Jews, the largest diaspora Jewish community in the world, was when it used its political power and moral force to help gain the freedom of the second largest diaspora community in the Former Soviet Union. Starting in the late 1980s, more than 1.7 million Jews were finally able to leave the FSU, the majority of whom came to Israel, while hundreds of thousands of others made their home in the U.S. Almost any Jew from the Former Soviet Union, liberal or conservative in political outlook, will immediately find resonance in Bernstein's arguments because woke ideology uses the exact same rhetoric used against us. If "lived experience" of the oppressed is the gold standard of evidence in today's world, then Americans should pay special attention to the lived experience of people who have labored under truly oppressive conditions in totalitarian countries. They are keenly aware of the difference between life in a totalitarian country and life in a democracy. And many, like me, are deeply uneasy about the ascent of woke ideology, which is reminiscent of the totalitarian ideology they grew up with.

The risk of woke ideology is not, of course, limited to the spread of antisemitism. It is a fundamental threat to the liberal idea in America. Just look at how many in this ideological movement erase the legacy of the great civil rights leader, Rev. Dr. Martin Luther King Jr. who was, after all, dedicated to broadening the borders of an inclusive, liberal society. For the proponents of this ideology, King's was a "passive" approach that perpetuates white hegemony. But that's only because their aims are not liberal. They seek to impose a view of the world and won't let others with different ideas and approaches even speak their minds because it benefits "the privileged" who are already exploiting society.

Unfortunately, woke ideology has succeeded in making many people too afraid to express their views. Surveys show that a majority of Americans prefer not to speak openly about their political perspectives. One of the personal costs of conceding to this ideology is a phenomenon we knew well in the Soviet Union—becoming a doublethinker, when people pretend to believe in something they don't. In the Soviet Union, doublethinkers did not become dissidents because it was too dangerous. They could have been killed. So they kept their critical opinions of the regime to themselves and lived in a constant state of self-censorship.

To be sure, the United States as a free country is the opposite to the Soviet Union. But we should not underestimate the dangers. The "cancel culture" in America today is just as capable of bullying people into silence and splitting their lives as any government agency. The difference is that no one will disappear you for saying the wrong thing. But that places the onus on people who have room to dissent. Unlike in the Soviet Union, in today's America you cannot blame a dictator for preventing you from speaking. No one is forcing you into doublethink. The freedom of expression depends only on the courage of your convictions. If liberal democracy in America is to survive and thrive, it depends on people taking such risks. Are you a doublethinker or not? If you're not a doublethinker, then don't be afraid to express your views.

As I have argued before, the difference between a "free society" and a "fear society" is whether you can go in the public square in the center of town and speak your mind. If you can express yourself without being punished, you are in a free society. If you are afraid to do so, you are in a fear society. I call this the "Town Square Test." To think that in a free America a postdoctoral student at Harvard would tell me, "I wanted very much to express my sympathy with Israel but knew that three professors I needed for career advancement would derail me," should send shock waves into the Jewish community and all lovers of freedom.

Indeed, this is an important moment for the American Jewish community. In my judgment, the role of the Jew is not to join forces with the ideological fads of the day, but to stand up for independent thought and the liberal principles on which the democracies of the world were founded. And that is exactly what the book of David Bernstein stands for. I hope that American Jews and others will give this book and its author a full and fair hearing. Woke ideology is genuinely dangerous for Jews, for society, and for the world. The courageous American Jewish community that unwaveringly advocated for and secured the release of Soviet Jews must be willing to stand up for the liberal values and the open society that they've helped build and benefited from.

"If liberty means anything at all it means the right to tell people what they do not want to hear."

—George Orwell

INTRODUCTION

Although American political liberals—many Jews among them—had no overarching theory about why some people had more power, money, or success than others until recently, we believed society had an obligation to help its less fortunate. Being politically liberal had always meant the pursuit of compassionate public policy (which, to be sure, didn't always produce the desired results), not about pontificating elaborate theories that purported to explain all privilege and all suffering. Today's Progressive ideologues, on the other hand, claim to know exactly why some people have more and others less: they insist that those who have are responsible for bringing about the deprivations of those who have not.

Most people I knew growing up and have worked with throughout my career were politically liberal and not particularly ideological. They just thought it was everyone's responsibility to help the less fortunate, no matter what the cause of the disparity. Today, some of those same people have joined the ranks of Progressive ideologues—the people with all the answers. In this book, I explain, from my personal and professional vantage point in the Jewish and political worlds, the origins of this seismic shift in political attitudes and its drastic repercussions, particularly for the Jewish community. I show the ways that woke ideology, well-meaning though it may be, fuels both antidemocratic sentiment and antisemitism, and I suggest a way out of this ideological morass.

A few words about terminology:

- I use the term "cancel culture," which describes the censorious trend that has taken hold in many institutions in American life and in the Jewish community, a trend that makes people afraid they will be ostracized [or worse] if they say the wrong thing or advance ideas at odds with woke thinking. Those who downplay cancel culture tend to refute the "cancel" part—i.e., "You haven't been fired for your views" ("…So shut up!)—but those critics overlook the term "culture," which suggests that it's not just the act of getting de-platformed at issue, but the pervasive fear of censure that intimidates people into silence.

- I generally stay away from the term Critical Race Theory (CRT) because CRT can be a valid theoretical lens and only becomes a problem when it ceases to be just a theory and ripens into dogma that aims to crowd out other perspectives.
- I use the terms "liberal," "liberalism," and "liberal values," by which I mean classical, small-L liberal values: freedom of expression, free speech, and civil liberties operating under the rule of law. A classical liberal today can be a political conservative devoted to "conserving" liberal and other traditional values as well as a political liberal devoted to the same set of principles. I use "political liberal" to describe people or ideas associated with a left-of-center public policy agenda (e.g., abortion rights, separation of church and state, enhanced government support for healthcare for those in need). Otherwise, I'm referring to the small-L, classical definition of the word.
- I use the term "postmodernism," a Twentieth century intellectual movement, which holds that knowledge is not objective but is socially constructed to maintain oppressive systems of power. In this conception, knowledge—what people think they know about the world—is constructed by powerful forces in society in a way that benefits the powerful. This "knowledge" is then accepted as true by society and perpetuated in how we talk about things. According to Postmodern theory, these oppressive power systems permeate everything but cannot easily be seen because they are deeply embedded in the discourse; they are like the air we breathe.[1]
- I use the terms "woke" and "woke ideology." To be sure, "woke" raises hackles; it's viewed by some as pejorative. I first heard the term from Progressive activists in 2016 who used it to describe

themselves and their work. They didn't regard it as pejorative then. In fact, "woke" has deep roots in the Black community's vernacular going all the way back to the 1930s, when Huddie Ledbetter (Leadbelly) coined the term, and it has been voiced in popular songs such as "Stay Woke" ever since. I use the term here because most people have at least a vague idea of what it means, and because it's such a precise exhortation to see—to be awoken to—hidden systems of oppression—one of the main claims of woke ideology. By "woke ideology," I mean the outgrowth of postmodernist thought that holds two core tenets: that bias and oppression are not just matters of individual attitude but are embedded in the very structures and systems of society, and that only those with lived experience of oppression have the insight to define oppression for the rest of society.[2] The second of the two tenets is referred to as "standpoint epistemology," the idea that knowledge is derived from one's position in the power structure. In this framework, knowledge is tied to identity and an individual's perceived position in society in relation to power. A Black person, for example, must be more knowledgeable about racism, a woman about misogyny, a disabled person about ableism, and so on. I maintain throughout the book that woke claims often have kernels of truth—bias can be and often is embedded in systems. And people who have been on the receiving end of bias and oppression often do have insights that others don't. The problem I identify in this book arises because woke ideology crowds out all alternative explanations and theoretical frameworks, thereby establishing itself as the one and only explanation for society's problems. In so doing, it shuts down liberal discourse and empowers radical voices.

In watching this ideology unfold (often in silent horror) over the course of more than three decades—seeing it emerge from a remote academic study to become an international post-colonialist movement, then a faddish campus ideology, then morph into corporate diversity programs, and from there to a dominant ideology in mainstream institutions including many Jewish organizations—I've come away with a central observation: Dogma begets ever more extreme dogma. The more we defer to an irrational set of beliefs, the more extreme and more dangerous those beliefs become over time. Each time an apex of craziness makes itself known, the ideology produces yet crazier manifestations, and its demands become more extreme. My book shows how the woke absurdities have piled on each other from the ideology's earliest form on campus to where we find ourselves today. I demonstrate that we are here, cowering in fear of being cancelled for saying the wrong thing, because we acquiesced—often in the name of empathy—to woke ideological demands. And if we remain where we are today, I argue, we will enable more and more hostility toward Jews, and undermine our democratic system.

As for its impact on the Jewish community, woke ideology short-circuits the deliberative process in Jewish organizations by making it impossible to discuss sensitive topics. Among other issues, woke ideology makes identifying problems and solutions to declining Jewish affiliation more difficult by insisting that such efforts are prejudicial and misogynistic. Woke ideology alienates many Jews with divergent political attitudes from Jewish institutions by treating their views as bigotry or by otherwise insisting that their politics are beyond the pale. And woke ideology inflames both anti-Israelism and antisemitism by spreading dogma that empowers extremists and antisemites.

I discuss these ill effects of woke ideology here, but I don't spill ink debating what constitutes antisemitism or rehashing the argument over at what point anti-Israelism crosses the line into antisemitism. Woke ideology foments both anti-Israelism and antisemitism, and for my purposes here, I'm not particularly concerned about some magical threshold where the former becomes the latter.

Critics of my and others' work opposing woke ideology often claim that the threat of rightwing extremism is several orders of magnitude higher than that of the left, and that liberal critics of woke ideology are misguided in focusing on such piddly claptrap. The threats on the right are indeed serious. But I don't live on the right, I live on the left. Congresswoman Marjorie Taylor Green, the Georgia Republican who promotes a white genocide theory among other conspiracies, has no influence in the Jewish community, but diversity guru Robin DiAngelo is steadily gaining ground. Francis Fukuyama argues that "these threats to liberalism are not symmetrical. The one coming from the right is more immediate and political; the one on the left is primarily cultural and therefore slower-acting."[3] Brookings Institution scholar Jonathan Rauch once likened the problem on the right to a heart attack and the problem on the left to a cancer. That sounds about right to me. Even if the threat to democracy is more serious on the right than on the left, that doesn't mean we shouldn't address the threat on the left. Someone has to fix the gaping pothole on your street even when there's a more serious water main break across town. I have zero influence in halting the heart attack on the right, but as a lifelong liberal, I do have standing—as well as a compelling interest—to check the cancer on the left.

In May of 2021, I founded the Jewish Institute for Liberal Values (JILV), a 501(c)(3) nonprofit dedicated to supporting liberal principles of free thought and expression, advancing viewpoint diversity, countering the imposition of woke ideology in the Jewish community, and highlighting and opposing the novel but unmistakable forms of antisemitism emerging from woke ideology. JILV's central strategy is to identify and recruit Jews who already share our concerns about the current illiberal moment and rising Progressive antisemitism, and to encourage them to stand up for liberal values and oppose this menacing form of Jew hatred. We've recruited hundreds of Jewish leaders and ordinary people into our work. But we still have much to do. I outline some additional strategies we must take to oppose rising antisemitism, advocate for small-L liberalism, and restore liberal values to the Jewish community and general society.

In the first part of the book (chapters 1–13) I share my observations on the growth of woke ideology and its capture of key American Jewish institutions. From my vantage point as a Jewish leader and professional advocate who has been on the front lines of many of the major political and ideological controversies of the day, I document woke ideology's ascent to dominance in the American Jewish community. I draw on personal experience to highlight woke ideology's multiple manifestations, its corruption of Jewish institutions, its assault on Jewish identity, and the spike in Progressive antisemitism it has provoked.

In the second part of the book (chapters 13–16), I identify a series of strategies to counter the onslaught of woke ideology and offer an alternative framework for Jewish advocacy and engagement. I urge the Jewish community to pivot from its customary support of an ideologically-motivated social justice platform to embrace a platform of liberal democracy, to assemble a new set of non-Jewish partners who share a commitment to democratic ideals, and to push back against the extremes on both ends of the ideological spectrum.

If I have a goal here beyond shedding light on acute threats to American society and the Jewish people, it's to inspire people who are nervous about speaking their minds publicly about woke ideology. Only when enough of us speak out will we change the discourse, face down these dangerous ideological forces, and put woke antisemitism in its proper place.

PART I

THE PROBLEM WITH WOKE IDEOLOGY

CHAPTER 1

GROWING UP JEWISH AND LIBERAL

I grew up a liberal in both senses of the word: I believed in the free expression of ideas and civil liberties, as the classical liberal does, and I supported causes such as abortion rights and government aid to the poor, as the political liberal does. Growing up Jewish in Columbus, Ohio, in the 1970s and '80s, every political liberal I knew was also a classical liberal. They felt as strongly about one's right to be wrong as they did that one could be very, very wrong. Today these two forms of liberalism have become disjoined. Many political liberals have traded in classical liberal values for what writer Wesley Yang calls the "successor ideology," commonly known as woke ideology. It's an ideology that claims to have the absolute truth about why there's disparity in the world and, hence, overrides the need for societal debate about such matters. It claims to be a successor to liberalism. In the name of justice, the ideology undercuts free discourse and foments antisemitism. It insinuates itself into institutions and changes their values and culture, often without ever firing a shot, mostly because those who oppose the ideology never bother to resist.

Growing up a civil libertarian

In 1981, when I was fourteen, my parents let me stay up late one night to watch the film *Skokie*. Based on actual events, the movie was about the American Nazi Party selecting the suburb Skokie, just north of Chicago, as the site of its next rally. Close to 40 percent of the suburb's population was Jewish, and many were Holocaust survivors. For the survivors, the prospect of the Nazi march was a terrifying evocation of the rise of the Nazi party in Germany. They opposed it with all their might. The American Civil Liberties Union (ACLU), represented by a Jewish attorney named David Goldberger, took up the cause of defending—on free speech grounds—the Nazis' right to march.

My mother, a Jew from Iraq, sided with the survivors. My father, a Jew of European descent and a civil libertarian, sided with those defending the Nazis' right to march. On an emotional level, I sympathized with the agony of the survivors who would re-live the trauma of the Nazi rise. But having absorbed the ethos of the American civil liberty tradition, it struck me even then that for America to be the kind of country where Nazis didn't come to power, it had to uphold its democratic principles. I was squarely with my dad and the First Amendment. If you didn't think Nazis—the very incarnation of evil—had the right to freedom of expression just like everyone else, then you didn't really support the First Amendment. The movie had such a profound impact on me that I thought I might eventually take up public interest law. Seven years later, when President George H. W. Bush lambasted his Democratic challenger Michael Dukakis as a "card-carrying member of the ACLU," I wanted to know where I could get one of those ACLU cards.

The ACLU of today, large swaths of which having embraced woke ideology, bears little resemblance to the organization that defended the Nazis' right to march in Skokie. In March 2022, former ACLU Executive Director Ira Glasser stated on *Real Time with Bill Maher* that "There is a requirement now for ACLU lawyers that before they take a case defending someone's free speech, they have to make sure that the speech doesn't offend or threaten other civil liberties values."[4] Of its nineteen policy priorities today, only one is dedicated to free speech.[5] Inasmuch as the ACLU only defends speech it approves of, it's no longer a civil liberties organization. It's merely a partisan vehicle upholding a favored set of policies or ideological preferences. This is what happens when venerable organizations supporting equal rights defer to the latest ideological fads and revile all alternative viewpoints at odds with the prevailing ideological orthodoxy. They lose their sense of purpose and organizational "soul." And that slouch to ideological acquiescence is precisely what I fear is happening in the Jewish world today, much of which is also abandoning its core principles. Today, if I had an ACLU card, I'd turn it in.

Growing up debating

From my early teens, my guy friends and I argued about politics, social issues, sports, and whether a single debit card works at every ATM machine. We argued about sex, which we knew very little about but expounded on with the authority of Dr. Ruth Westheimer, the Jewish German-American sex therapist and Holocaust survivor, whose show we watched on the cable TV Health Channel on Friday evenings after Shabbat dinner. We argued about God's existence, free will, and trees falling in forests. We nearly came to blows over whether the 1954 Cleveland Indians would beat today's World Series champ (no, they wouldn't). Since my freshman year in college, I've been on both sides of more arguments over the efficacy and constitutionality of school vouchers than I care to remember. None of us ever took the disagreements personally. In fact, these arguments sealed our friendships.

When I had kids of my own, I began teaching them to construct an argument as soon as they could speak in complete sentences. I instituted Shabbat dinner debates, which have now been going on for twenty years, though the dinners have unfortunately become less frequent. On Friday night, I raise an issue for discussion. The topic can be anything from "Should parents monitor their kids' social media?" to "Is it the government's responsibility to pay for college?" Very often my two children and two stepchildren—now all in their teens or older—request a different topic, such as "Should gender be abolished?" (yes, that's a thing) or "Do video games cause violence?" and I typically relent because the topic doesn't really matter. My role, much to their frustration, is devil's advocate. No matter the issue, I always take the opposing view. "Video game violence may not matter in France, where no one owns a gun, but it obviously creates a culture of violence among American youth," I once announced to a dinner table of teenage gamers who stared like they wanted to shoot me in the face. My children beg for the big reveal—my actual perspective—which I duly withhold until I feel satisfied that they have fully fleshed out their positions. As time has passed, they have begun to proffer coherent arguments. My wife raised my teenage stepson to value critical thinking above all else. No slouch in the disputative arts, he once caught himself committing a dastardly logical fallacy in one of our dinner table discussions: "The only reason cinema attendance has gone down is that Disney has taken ownership and ruined all the good film series." My wife and I fell silent. "I know," he conceded. "No shitty arguments allowed." I grew up learning by arguing. It is heartbreaking to me when Jewish leaders and organizations stifle legitimate debate in the name of social justice.

Growing up in an immigrant family

Another important aspect of my upbringing was being raised by Jews from Iraq—my mother, grandmother, and extended family, who lived two hours away in Cincinnati, whom we saw frequently. My mother came directly to the United States in 1963, and a couple of years later married my third-generation Ashkenazi father. When I was three, my grandmother came from Baghdad and moved in with us. Three years later my grandmother's sister and her fourteen-year-old son Sam also both immigrated from Iraq to live with us, and took my brother's bedroom for three years. The house bustled with high-pitched laughter and arguments laced in colorful Arabic swear words, punctuated by a screeching parrot named Bibi. I spoke to my grandmother and great aunt in a Jewish dialect of Arabic. My father, who spoke no Arabic, often took refuge in the bedroom.

The Iraqi side of my family always worshiped America. When I was a young child, my mother would refer to Iraq as "back home." When she finally became a citizen in 1971, however, she announced that Iraq was no longer her home, and she vowed never to use that phrase again. Just a few months after my mother arrived in the US at the University of Cincinnati, President John F. Kennedy was shot and killed in Dallas. My mother told me that her first thought, having experienced multiple coups in Iraq, was that tanks would soon roll down the streets of Cincinnati, dragging the dead bodies of the President's family members and advisors. Needless to say, that didn't happen. And my mother got a lesson in how politics works in a democratic society.

As much as they loved America, most of my Iraqi relatives didn't entirely grasp what makes a democracy tick. "Why can't you just expel those people from the country, if they are making trouble?" they asked. In the end, however, it didn't matter that our Iraqi-born relatives weren't schooled in the latest political doctrines or the finer points of democracy. They were focused on making a living, not running for office. But like many of the immigrants who come to the United States from repressive dictatorships, they still appreciate the fruits of democracy. My Iraqi relatives know that in Afghanistan, the Taliban were the bad guys and the Americans were a force for good. They never went in for political word games—played on both sides of the political spectrum—that serve to muddle the differences between freedom and actual oppression. This basic distinction between a democracy and an authoritarian regime is something I think about when I hear right-wing populists and woke ideologues alike pretend that our hard-won democratic institutions are a mask for tyranny or oppression. They clearly don't know what it's like to live under a truly oppressive regime.

Growing up with antisemitism

In March 1977, in Penick v. Columbus Board of Education, Circuit Court Judge Robert Duncan ruled that beginning in 1909, the Columbus, Ohio, Board of Education knowingly kept white and African American students apart from each other.[6] And so began bussing, the policy of shuttling Black students to white-majority schools, and vice versa. My parents firmly supported the decision, though they worried I would be bussed to another school far away. Upon hearing the announcement, my fifth-grade teacher Mrs. Davis—Olive Oyl's evil twin and an avowed racist—informed the class that she didn't want to teach all those "Black troublemakers," thereby humiliating the one Black girl in the room, who started crying. Mrs. Davis doubled down: "She needs to hear this!" I boiled with anger and disgust but didn't have the maturity or courage to say or do anything about it.

In the wake of *Pennick*, many Jews I knew moved out of the east side of Columbus, where I lived, to the nearby Bexley school district, where the majority of the Jewish community still resided, to avoid what they perceived as the likely diminution of the schools, not to mention their property values. Not my family. We stayed firmly put. In 1979, at the age of twelve, I entered Yorktown Junior High School, which had been demographically transformed overnight. I wasn't shocked by being put into the same classes with Black kids from the inner city—I was shocked by being put into the same classes with blue-collar white kids who had grown up with few, if any, Jews. Plenty of them were antisemitic bullies. But I cannot recall a single instance of a direct antisemitic insult from a Black student in middle or upper school. And while I know that some Black leaders now regret the degeneration of Black communities and schools wrought by desegregation (Harvard sociologist Orlando Patterson argues contrarily that integration is essential for the well-being and mobility of Black people[7]), I will forever value the experience of going to school with Black kids, several of whom I got to know and befriended.

I hated high school. When I got to ninth grade at Walnut Ridge High, the taunts from white students—supposedly made in good fun—got worse. Some threw pennies at my feet. "You're such a fucking Jew!" they would say. They drew swastikas in my books. One nerdy guy, trying to gain popularity points, once threw a bagel during marching band practice and told me to fetch it while everyone laughed. "Go get it, Jew!" No doubt being a socially awkward late bloomer with attention deficit disorder didn't help, but it was my Jewishness they latched on to. After one particularly odious coin-tossing incident in the school hallway, a popular kid named Jamie tapped me on the shoulder on the way to class and whispered, "No one knows this, but my father is Jewish." Jamie meant the comment, no doubt, as a modest show of support, but I felt intense rage at his cowardice in hiding his identity.

As I grew in stature and confidence, the taunts lessened, but I couldn't wait to get out of Walnut Ridge. I enrolled at Ohio State during what would have been my senior year in high school, finishing up my remaining high school credits over the summer. Some years later in college, I faced a different kind of antisemitism coming from left-wing figures and groups, which was both similar to and different from the bullying in high school. The antisemitism from the left was often couched in euphemisms such as "Zionists" and was expressed in ideological terms, in contrast to the churlish mockery favored by high school bullies and the brazen acts of violence committed by hardened white supremacists.

***

Being a civil libertarian, as most Jews were; loving debate, as many Jews did; experiencing antisemitism, as most Jews have; and growing up in a patriotic immigrant home full of gratitude for America, as nearly all immigrant families did, I was naturally predisposed to oppose woke ideology because it mocks civil liberties, which some woke ideologues view as a function of white supremacy; it stifles open debate and discourse; it fuels left-wing antisemitism; and it views America as an oppressive state. Unless I became an entirely different person, as a few of the people I know apparently did, I was destined to oppose the imposition of this ascending dogma.

CHAPTER 2

POLITICAL CORRECTNESS COMES TO CAMPUS

Early Social Justice Warriors

In the late 1980s and early 1990s, when I was in college and then graduate school, I experienced the early iterations of woke ideology then known as "political correctness." In the fall of 1987, I had just come back from a year traveling and studying in Israel, trying to meet Israeli girls, and becoming enthralled by philosophers such as Martin Buber and Franz Rosenzweig. When I returned to Ohio State in the fall of 1986, I promptly gave up on my computer science major and decided—much to my mother's chagrin—to study philosophy. I also became a leading pro-Israel activist in college, later serving on the national Jewish student leadership board called "The Secretariate."

In the spring of 1987, I attended my first national convention of Hillel, the center for Jewish student life, in Washington, DC, with other Jewish students from around the country. Some of the students I encountered were very different from the mild-mannered Jews I grew up with in Columbus. These students were the "social justice warriors" of my generation, though we didn't call them that then: women with unshaved legs and armpits, wearing flowing floral skirts and sandals, and hippie-wannabe guys sporting pins with such sayings as "Celebrate

Difference." One female student with unruly frizzy brown hair wrapped in a red bandana, who went to the University of Wisconsin, had a small button on her backpack that read "PC." "What's that mean?" I asked. She rolled her eyes and declared without a trace of irony "politically correct, like we have the correct view on political issues." While such sentiment was surely a common conceit of youth, I had never met anyone who so brazenly declared their correctness, let alone boasted about it on a pin, but that kind of self-righteousness turned out to be a new normal.

That evening, the students gathered in a circle to hear an Israeli storyteller regale us with tales of Ethiopian Jews traveling on foot for thousands of miles under the most perilous conditions from Ethiopia to Sudan, where they were picked up in the darkness by a plane arranged by the Israeli Mossad. I was mesmerized by his account of "Operation Moses," conjuring the miraculous "ingathering of the exiles" prophesied in the Bible. "There were two beautiful Ethiopian women standing in the corner, like statues," the story-teller told us. I knew what he meant, having seen for myself such stunning Ethiopian women with their strong features, their high cheekbones, wafting through the streets of Jerusalem. Immediately a group of five leftist students sitting on the edge of a table outside the circle burst out heckling. "Would you have called Ethiopian men statues?" one woman shouted out. The story-teller paused to think. "Yes, I would have," he said. "Bullshit!" blurted another student. Two of them then walked out of the room, followed several seconds later by the other three because, in their view, the story-teller had objectified the women. Their future woke kids might have accused him of "exotifying" them as well.

Who were these students with all the answers? I wondered. When I got back to the Ohio State campus, my friend Dan, a skinny Jewish guy with long curly brown hair and John Lennon glasses who spent time with the progressive crowd, was wearing a button on his Levi's jean jacket that read "Men Rape, Men Can Stop Rape." Reminded of the hecklers at the Hillel conference, I asked him mockingly "What the fuck is that? Are you saying all men rape because a few men rape?" Political correctness had arrived at Ohio State.

Feminism Then and Now

In those days feminism, more than racism, was the progressive topic *du jour*. A shy young woman named Wendy, sitting on the couch in the social room at Ohio State Hillel, had a book on the coffee table called *Intercourse* written by the second-wave feminist author Andrea Dworkin, an imposing, indignant crusader against pornography. "Can I see that?" I asked. "That's a book for my women's study class," she said softly, turning red. For Dworkin, male-female sexual intercourse was inherently an act of violence and patriarchy. My friend Michael grabbed the book from me, opened it to a random page, and began reading a passage. "The woman must be reduced to being this sexual object to be pleasing to men who will then, and only then, want to fuck her; once she is made inferior in this way, she is sensual to men and attracts them to her, and a man's desire for her."[8] "That's so hot!" Michael exclaimed, further embarrassing Wendy. We took turns reading passages out loud, undoubtedly not in the spirit Dworkin intended. In September of 2018, at a meeting at Bard College, I learned from a prominent contemporary of Dworkin's in the feminist movement that Dworkin's male partner, John Stoltenberg, had foresworn sexual intercourse out of respect for Dworkin's philosophy.

So the next quarter, I signed up for a women's study course in the hopes of engaging with some of the absurdities I encountered in the book. I suppose I thought it would be fun to argue with the people in the women's studies class. I was used to being the class gadfly, unafraid of conflict, especially in classes that taught an unfavorable one-sided view of Israel, which was then amid the first intifada and coming off the debacle of the Lebanon war. By then, Israel was no longer the darling of the left. As contentious as these Middle East Studies classes could be, the Women's Studies class was on another level. A relentlessly humorless woman who reeked of contempt, the professor waxed indignant about male domination and objectification of women. I once tried to challenge her, but she cut me off with "I will not have you change the subject of this class!" This was not an open discussion or a liberal education in any sense of the word. In my philosophy classes, challenging the readings and the professor was *de rigueur*. Not so, I discovered, in Women's Studies.

"I'm going to flunk this class," I told Michael. "There's no way I can write what she wants, and there's no way she won't flunk me if I write what I want." On his advice, I dropped the class. But it wasn't lost upon me that it was somehow acceptable for a professor of Women's Studies to teach her own point of view as gospel and to shut down anyone who didn't agree. This was indoctrination, I thought, not education. Ironically, many of these same "second-wave" feminist thinkers have now found themselves on the other side of the culture wars, having been labelled "Trans Exclusionary Radical Feminists" (TERFs) by radical trans activists, for the thought crime of clinging to the category of "woman." The names of the departments at universities are being changed from Women's Studies to Gender Studies. It's amusing to think these same radical feminists may now side with me on gender-related issues. They're the latest victims of an ideology they helped set in motion.

As disenchanted as I was by the experience, I had been reading various feminist authors and fell under the influence of more moderate feminist thinkers, such as the Orthodox Jewish feminist Blu Greenberg, who carved out a place for women in the Jewish tradition. Brandeis University feminist professor Sylvia Barack Fishman gave a talk at another Hillel conference about the Jewish American Princess (JAP) stereotype, a popular notion in those days of spoiled Jewish women who spent their daddies' money and came to college only to get married. I was intrigued. This stereotype, she insisted, demeaned women. She gave several examples of how antisemites used the JAP stereotype to make derogatory accusations about Jewish women. She showed us a pamphlet written by Cornell students called "JAPS be gone, a guide to extermination." It was obscenely antisemitic. I remembered the case a few years back of Steven Steinberg, who killed his wife by stabbing her twenty-six times. Steinberg was acquitted after his defense depicted his dead wife in court as an overbearing "Jewish American Princess" whose behavior provoked her husband into murdering her.[9] Later that quarter, I wrote an opinion piece in the Ohio State newspaper, *The Lantern*, calling upon my fellow Buckeyes to cease using the JAP stereotype. It was the talk of campus for a good two days. People I didn't know stopped me, as I walked the crisscrossing paths of the Oval in the center of campus on my way to class, and told me they loved the article. A female friend told me that the article was taped to the wall of the Sigma Delta Tau (SDT) house, a Jewish sorority we jokingly referred to as "seldom datem twice." I would have called it "Jappy" before I knew better.

Justifying Jew Hatred

I confronted a different kind of antisemitism than what I experienced in high school. I had become a campus pro-Israel advocate, which back then meant planning pro-Israel programs with speakers, passing out propaganda, and arguing with Arab students about who started the Six Day War. In the fall of 1989, Rabbi Meir Kahane, the American-born Orthodox Rabbi and extremist who called for the expulsion of Israel's Palestinian population—a position that got him kicked out of Israel's parliament—announced he was coming to campus to deliver a speech. He requested the social hall at Hillel. The request, of course, sparked an uproar among Jewish students. I was a member of the Jewish Student Activities Board, which debated and ultimately voted against allowing Kahane to speak at the Hillel building. That infuriated Kahane and his local supporters. Prior to Kahane's arrival, in an interview in *The Lantern*, I made it very clear that I rejected Kahane's extremism and expressed my pride in the student board's decision. Incensed by my comments, the gray-bearded Kahane took to the podium at the student union, where I stood in the background, too curious to stay away, and railed against me with a pronounced tic as a "pathetic, self-hating Jew." "Bernstein is no Jewish leader," he growled. I basked in the attention.

A few days later, I saw fliers posted around campus that an equally notorious Black nationalist and extremist, Stokely Carmichael a.k.a. Kwame Ture, was coming to Ohio State. Carmichael traded in extreme antisemitic rhetoric. I had read his comments that "a Jew would say the only good Nazi is a dead Nazi. When you condemn Nazis you don't condemn Germans, you condemn a political philosophy. Zionists try to make their philosophy into a particular people. I'm against Zionism. The only good Zionist is a dead Zionist."[10] Undeterred, I went to the event alone. True to form, Carmichael railed against America, the colonialist West and, of course, the "Zionists." He even stated in his speech that he understood there were Zionist infiltrators in the room, and then repeated the calumny "the only good Zionist is a dead Zionist," putting me, a known campus activist, at risk. Curiously, I don't remember being particularly afraid for my physical wellbeing but rather angry at the applause in the room for Carmichael's demeaning tirade.

I later found out that Carmichael, unlike Kahane, had been paid to speak by the University, in this case by its Black Studies department. I was apoplectic. While I had no problem with Carmichael speaking, I had a major problem with the university paying for a known antisemite to spread his hatred. I gave another interview to *The Lantern*, stating that "Just as I would have opposed the university sponsoring Kahane, I oppose the university sponsoring another known racist in Carmichael." None of this, of course, endeared me to either the radical Black students who in those days went by "Afrocentric," or the mostly Arab anti-Israel students on campus.

A few days after the Carmichael event, as I sat dipping my pita at a table in Ali Baba's, a Syrian restaurant on campus with delicious pomegranate-infused baba ghanouj, two Black activist students involved with the Carmichael event walked into the restaurant and ordered. We glanced and nodded at each other, and I invited them to take a seat at my table. We immediately began to argue about Carmichael's various antisemitic rants. It must have gone on for ten minutes when two Arab students sitting at the table next to us, overhearing the discussion, chimed in even more crudely than the Black activists I was trying to win over. "You Jews take control wherever you are, America, Palestine, Europe, it doesn't matter. You are the world's oppressors. That's why everyone wants you dead." I was unmoved. I had heard such sentiment before. Maybe, I thought, the Black students would now get my point about the vulnerability that Jews face. I looked at the faces of my Black interlocutors, who smiled and nodded in agreement with the Arab students. "Yup," one blurted out. Antisemitism, I learned in college, didn't just come from white, blue collar guys throwing pennies at my shoes.

Arguments for the Sake of Heaven

When I graduated from Ohio State in 1990, I returned to Israel to spend some time at Ohr Somayach Yeshiva, a place of learning for

Jews studying Jewish texts with a mix of young Jews like me wanting to learn more about Orthodox Judaism, another cohort I'll call "seekers" who were inclined to accept a whole new way of life and belief system in one sitting, and the already fervently committed. A strictly Orthodox "black hat" Yeshiva, Ohr Somayach was probably not the right place for my restless and doubting mind, but the Yeshiva had the added benefit of being free of cost as long as I stuck to the program. Studying there was both gratifying and frustrating. On the one hand, there was a limit to what I could publicly question. At Ohr Samayach, the Torah was given to the Jewish people by God at Mt. Sinai, full stop. You could question within the tradition but not the authority of the tradition itself. The Yeshiva didn't even keep a copy of *The Guide for the Perplexed* by the much-lionized medieval physician and philosopher Moses Maimonides (known as "The Rambam"). *The Guide* was Maimonides' attempt to help curiously minded medieval Jews navigate their doubts about Jewish tradition in the face of the appeal of Greek philosophy. But some authorities interpreted the book as challenging the tradition itself by citing the skeptics' arguments. According to my college Jewish philosophy professor, Tamar Rudavsky, Maimonides was a master of both Judaism and Greek philosophy. She placed a wheel on a five-foot-long wire and had a student grasp the other end of the wire. If the wheel, rolling down the wire, fell to the left, Maimonides secretly sided with Judaism. If it fell to the right, he secretly sided with Greek philosophy. The wheel fell to the right. "See?" Rudavsky said jocularly. "Greek philosophy." I wanted, like Maimonides, to wrestle with both Judaism and philosophy and discover for myself which side of the wire I fell off.

Ohr Somayach inculcated us with Maimonides' *Mishneh Torah*, his definitive work codifying Jewish law, but shielded us from his manifest intellectual dilemmas. This frustrated me to no end. On the other hand, in studying Talmud—the Jewish oral tradition featuring religious and ethical disputes by rabbis—we were taught a rigorous thought process that trained the mind for all manner of intellectual pursuits, but was ultimately designed to satisfy our intellectual curiosity within the tradition's framework. That same thought process, I later came to appreciate, provided the tools for me and others to question what I considered the more dogmatic aspects of the Jewish tradition. Notwithstanding the Yeshiva's best efforts, one's mind didn't have to confine itself to the specified parameters.

On my first visit to the Yeshiva's Beit Midrash—the house of study where men sit face-to-face in pairs, studying Talmud together—I was minding my own business when one older man studying with a partner literally jumped out of his seat and started screaming and wildly gesticulating at the other. I couldn't believe it. I thought we were in something akin to a library, where people were expected to speak in hushed tones, if at all. Not one of the other men quietly studying so much as flinched. I sat down with my Talmud tutor to start deciphering the Aramaic, wondering if the maniac two tables away might soon again erupt. The Talmudic tract I was studying laid out the moral reasoning of who is responsible if one man's ox gores another man's calf. The purpose of this pedagogy was not to impart the facts around the ox and the calf, but rather to instill that critical thought process. Five minutes into the lesson, another man flew off the handle at his "Chavruta" partner, yelling and stomping, "he's *Patur* [exempt]!" In the Beit Midrash, such emotional interludes were par for the course.

Debate is so central to Jewish life that it is enshrined in the Mishna, the foundational texts of the Jewish oral tradition, in the concept of *Makhloket l'shem shamayim*—"arguments for the sake of heaven." Such was the ongoing dispute between Rabbis Hillel and Shammai, heads of two competing schools of thought. Legend has it that for several years the houses of Shammai and Hillel vehemently disagreed on a specific point of law. Ultimately, the Divine voice intervened and proclaimed: "Both these and those are the words of the living God. However, the law is in accordance with the opinion of Beit Hillel." The reason the law ultimately sided with Hillel, the tradition tells us, was that Hillel cited both its own statements and the statements of Shammai, possibly the first instance of "steel-manning"—presenting the strongest possible version of an opponent's argument—in recorded history.

This tradition of debate for the sake of heaven, which is central to my identity as a Jew, is worth protecting and nurturing. But it is being threatened by people who think they have all the answers. For woke ideologues, all debate over social issues is over and everyone should fall in line with the prescribed dogma. And it became clear to me, as they gained ground and the ideology spread, that dogma begets ever more extreme forms of dogma.

CHAPTER 3

WELCOME BACK TO HISTORY

High Hopes

After a brief stint working on the Clinton-Gore campaign in 1992, I went to work in October 1993 for the Jewish Community Relations Council of Greater Washington, the Jewish advocacy arm of the Washington, DC, Jewish community. Just a few weeks before I started the new job, Israeli Prime Minister Yitzhak Rabin and PLO chief Yasser Arafat shook hands on the White House lawn and signed the Oslo Accords, laying out incremental steps for the parties to achieve peace and Palestinian statehood. International TV news coverage featured scenes powerful enough to make a dove out of a hawk: joyous images of young Palestinians, who had previously thrown rocks and Molotov cocktails at Israeli soldiers, handing their adversaries olive branches. The week of the signing, in DC, I ran into a former nemesis from my days at Ohio State, an American-born Palestinian named Amir. He had once called me a "semi-skilled Zionist propagandist" in *The Lantern,* which I regarded as a pretty good line. Amir was now a well-dressed legal associate working for a top DC firm. "This is a wonderful moment," he said to me. "May there be peace in our time." I replied, "*Inshallah,*" the Arabic word for "May it be God's will." The signing of the Accords, we were told by the experts, unleashed forces that would inexorably bring about peace. According to Dennis Ross, Special Envoy for Middle East Peace, who played an instrumental role in the agreement and in future peace talks, Israeli-Palestinian peace was "inevitable."[11]And so it felt in those heady days.

The promising outlook for peace in the Middle East came on the heels of the collapse of the former Soviet Union, which had released from captivity millions of mostly educated Soviet Jews who were now able to migrate to Israel, the US, and Europe. Israelis and American Jews rose to the occasion to welcome and integrate these talented but often traumatized emigres. Both countries were better off for it. This wave of immigrants lessened Israel's long-term demographic problems and strengthened its economy with hundreds of thousands of highly educated workers and entrepreneurs. The dissolution of the Soviet Union also meant, of course, that America was now the sole global superpower and a stabilizing force in a "New World Order."

In 1992, the renowned American political scientist Francis Fukuyama came out with his highly influential but sadly mistaken book *The End of History and the Last Man*, in which he convincingly argued that with the ascendancy of Western liberal democracy and the dissolution of the Soviet Union, humanity had reached "the end-point of mankind's ideological evolution and the universalization of Western liberal democracy as the final form of human government."[12] Around that same time, Charles Krauthammer wrote in *Foreign Affairs* what turned out to be the more trenchant analysis that the collapse of the Soviet Union "marks a unique historical phenomenon, which might be called the moment of unipolarity....The multipolar world to which we are headed, in which power will emanate from Berlin and Tokyo, Beijing and Brussels, as well as Washington and Moscow, is struggling to be born. The transition between these two worlds is now, and it won't last long."[13]

Fukuyama's optimism and Krauthammer's realism were both in the air, but many—me included—fell for the "End of History" thesis. The supposed triumph of liberal democracy in the 1990s was good news for the Jews. The impending Israeli-Palestinian peace was good news for the Jews. The end of the cold war was good news for the Jews. The thriving economy under Clinton was good news for the Jews. The decline in antisemitism evident from various public surveys was good news for the Jews. We delighted in all the good news.

In this favorable external environment, the Jewish community turned inward to address the rising challenge of assimilation. Two Jewish population surveys, one in 1990 and the other in 1992, showed a steep rise in intermarriage rates.[14] Non-Orthodox Jews were marrying non-Jews to the tune of 50 percent, sending shockwaves through the Jewish world about a perceived threat to "Jewish survival." Studies also showed that intermarried families were far less likely to be active in Jewish life and that the non-Jewish spouse rarely converted to Judaism.[15] Jewish groups desperately sought new ways of strengthening "Jewish continuity," a politically correct euphemism at the time for promoting inmarriage among Jews.

While good for Jewish security, the decline in antisemitism posed a challenge to Jewish continuity. Could Jewish identity survive and thrive in such an open society? French existentialist Jean-Paul Sartre argued in his 1946 essay "The Antisemite and the Jew" that the Jew would not exist but for the antisemite. "If the Jew did not exist, the anti-Semite would invent him," he wrote.[16] While most Jews would deny Sartre's assertion, and insist that Jews possess a vibrant moral and spiritual tradition that didn't require antisemitism for its continued existence, many of us also privately asked ourselves if we could be so sure Sartre wasn't correct. If antisemitism precipitously declined, might Jews stop caring about being Jewish and simply marry themselves out of existence?

In 1997, I became Washington regional director of the American Jewish Committee, the vaunted global Jewish advocacy organization headquartered in New York with offices around the world. Early on, I had lunch with my counterpart, David Friedman, the regional director of the Anti-Defamation League, the civil rights and hate monitoring group. I insisted that antisemitism was no longer a major factor in American Jewish life, and that Jewish organizations should focus instead on bolstering Jewish continuity and securing Israel's place in the world. Despite being on the path to peace, Israel was still relatively isolated in international bodies and roundly condemned at UN meetings, I pointed out. Friedman was incredulous. "If you saw what comes across my desk every day, you wouldn't say that," he shot back. "Antisemitism is getting worse." Till then, I'd been pretty sure that the world's oldest hatred didn't have a future in a prosperous and liberal American society. Jews were safe, I thought. In any case, an age with little antisemitism would surely put John Paul Sartre's Jewish survival thesis to the test.

The End of Peace

My optimism, of course, turned out to be illusory, a short-lived respite from harsh external realities that history would ultimately impose. In July of 2000, the Camp David peace process unraveled after the parties couldn't reach an agreement on a two-state solution. President Clinton laid the blame squarely at the feet of Yasser Arafat. Arafat desperately wanted to change the narrative. Two months later, Israeli opposition leader Ariel Sharon brazenly visited the Temple Mount—a site holy to Jews, Christians, and Muslims—as a show of political force in opposition to Israeli Prime Minister Ehud Barak's concessions in the peace process. Sharon was sending a message to the Israeli public, deeply disappointed that Palestinians would not accept their best offer, that Sharon would protect Israeli interests, particularly its sovereignty over its capital, Jerusalem. Israelis, who—in preparation for a new, more peaceful era—had stripped themselves of their sustaining myths by acknowledging their fair share of the culpability in the origins of the conflict, were now unilaterally exposed and became deeply cynical. Palestinians, who had been sold a bill of goods by their leaders about what was truly offered to them at Camp David, were ready to pick up where the first intifada left off. It was a powder keg, and Arafat lit the match.

Distraught at the failure to reach peace, most American Jewish leaders couldn't immediately foresee how the renewed conflict would ignite a very different kind of conflict in the American Jewish community. It didn't take long for history to smack them in the face. The campaign to delegitimize Israel, and American Jewish support for the Jewish state, was in no time back in full swing. "After eight years of Oslo," I wrote in the *Washington Jewish Week* in May of 2003, "many in the Jewish community were simply not prepared to resume a posture that was at once familiar, yet distant—defending Israel's right to self-defense in a largely unsympathetic world. Jewish students, many of whom had never seen a protest in their lives, were caught totally flat-footed. When the violence first broke out, Muslims and Arab American groups held a series of boisterous rallies on numerous campuses that shook the campus community to its core."[17]

Postcolonialism and the Jews

One of the key moments in this new-old reality came in September 2001, when the World Conference against Racism, Racial Discrimination, Xenophobia and Related Intolerance took place in Durban, South Africa. The goal of the landmark conference was to explore effective methods to eradicate racial discrimination, and promote awareness of the global fight against intolerance. The conference, however, immediately descended into an anti-Jewish, anti-Israel hate fest, prompting both Israel and the United States to pull their delegations. Some conference participants renewed the slanderous charge that "Zionism is racism." At the conference, the Arab Lawyers Union passed out booklets containing images of Jews with blood-dripping fangs.[18] Friends of mine who were part of various Jewish delegations from the US—a number of them dyed-in-the-wool progressives—were completely shell-shocked and felt threatened by participants shouting them down at every turn.

The UN marked the twentieth anniversary of this disgraceful episode in September of 2021, not to express the requisite remorse, but to celebrate its supposed achievements. The Durban conference was a watershed moment for Jews around the world: a stark reminder that deliverance from the forces of history was not yet in the offing. The world's oldest hatred was alive and well, not just in the remnants of an unreconstructed Eastern Europe or the aggrieved masses of the Third World, but among the cosmopolitan classes of the West. Yet few American Jews understood or addressed a basic question about this revival of antisemitism: What was the underlying ideology driving the Jew-hatred at Durban? And, twenty years later, with a resurgence of left-wing antisemitism in the US and Europe, many still haven't figured out how a variant of that same ideological virus generates antisemitism today.

In the wake of the Durban conference, journalist Jonathan Rosen wrote a widely-circulated essay in *New York Times Magazine* about the "New Antisemitism," which captured the sentiment of many Jews, including myself. "I have been reminded, in ways too plentiful to ignore, about the role Jews play in the fantasy life of the world," Rosen stated. "Singling out Israel made of a modern nation an archetypal villain—Jews were the problem and the countries of the world were figuring out the solution."[19] There was, however, not a word in Rosen's article, or anywhere else, about the underlying ideology plaguing the Durban conference—one with which many of the Westerners and even Jews in attendance no doubt sympathized, if not outright supported. The debacle at Durban was an expression of postcolonialism: a critical academic study turned dogma, highlighting the legacy of colonialism, focusing on the human consequences of the exploitation of colonized people and lands. Postcolonialism came to be regarded by an activist community as a complete and inviolable explanation for why some countries flourish and others languish: the haves caused the deprivations of the have-nots—full stop. Any other explanation, particularly any that focused on cultural differences between various countries and regions, came to be regarded as racist and beyond the pale of legitimate discourse. The "Declaration and Programme of Action" of the Durban conference made its ideological orientation clear:

> We recognize that colonialism has led to racism, racial discrimination, xenophobia and related intolerance, and that Africans and people of African descent, and people of Asian descent and indigenous peoples were victims of colonialism and continue to be victims of its consequences.... We further regret that the effects and persistence of these structures and practices have been among the factors contributing to lasting social and economic inequalities in many parts of the world today.[20]

Of course, no other factor for disparity, such as regional cultural differences, was ever entertained. For good measure, the Declaration, in addressing the Israel-Palestinian issue, added, "We recognize the right of refugees to return voluntarily to their homes and properties in dignity and safety, and urge all States to facilitate such return." Such a policy, if adopted, would open the floodgates to millions of Palestinian descendants of refugees, change the demographic makeup of the country, and ultimately lead to eradication of the Jewish state.

Like all intellectual monopolies, postcolonialism denies the validity of other explanations, and in its certitude becomes an illiberal and dangerous source of extremism and hate. The ideology does, of course, contain a modicum of truth—the horrors of colonialism do contribute to some of today's global disparities. The proponents of postcolonialism, however, completely paper over the highly successful Asian countries that were once colonies, and what their achievements say about the varieties of long-term impacts of colonial rule. In simplistically dividing the world into oppressors and oppressed, postcolonialism holds successful nations morally culpable and struggling nations morally pure. And in insisting on this perverse binary, the ideology enables the expression of the usual resentment and ill-will toward Jews and Israel, both of whom have succeeded in their respective environments.

Talking about the antisemitism at Durban without reference to post-colonialist ideology was like talking about the attacks of September 11th without reference to extreme Islamist ideology. We should have grasped the underlying problem then: "It's the ideology, stupid." Fast-forward twenty years, and we see the same political dynamic—not in a remote international conference of NGOs and diplomats, but in multiple mainstream American institutions, including higher education, K–12 schools, corporations, the law, medicine, nonprofits, and even scientific research. Woke ideology is postcolonialism applied to the domestic scene in Western countries, neatly dividing people into victimizers and victims. And just like the post-Durban reckoning, those concerned about the resurgence of antisemitism today largely fail to understand and name the animating ideology, one that most assuredly inflames left-wing antisemitism.

The violence and political turmoil after the collapse of Camp David in 2000 constituted a watershed moment for American Jews: a realization that the messiah was not coming any time soon. The radical ideologies of the twentieth century had not, in fact, succumbed to liberalism. As the Israeli singer Shalom Hanoch voiced in the wake of the crash of the Israeli stock market in 1983 in his song "Waiting for the Messiah," "the Messiah is not coming, nor he is calling on the phone." History was back upon us with a vengeance and apparently here to stay.

CHAPTER 4

A NEW 'DIVERSITY' TAKES SHAPE

An Uneasy Relationship

During my early years at the American Jewish Committee in the late 1990s and early 2000s—before and after the collapse of the Israeli-Palestinian peace process and the eruption of violence—I focused on strengthening intergroup relations, especially ties between Blacks and Jews. Black-Jewish relations had fallen on tough times since the high point of civil rights collaboration in the early 1960s. The image of Rev. Martin Luther King Jr. and Rabbi Abraham Joshua Heschel locking arms with other civil rights leaders in the 1965 voter rights march from Selma, Alabama, to Montgomery, the state capital, was forever seared into the collective memory of the American Jewish community. Liberal Jews yearned to reconnect with the Black community in common purpose. Collaboration between Black and Jewish leaders was not merely symbolic; it was institutional. Many of the professional and volunteer leaders in mainstream civil rights organizations, such as the NAACP, were Jews. The offices of the Leadership Conference of Civil Rights—the DC-based umbrella organization under whose auspices civil rights laws were drafted—were run by a Jewish professional, Arnold Aronson, of an organization I previously headed, the National Jewish Community Relations Advisory Council (later renamed Jewish Council for Public Affairs), and housed in the same offices as several

Jewish organizations, such as the Reform Action Committee of Reform Judaism and the American Jewish Congress.

The role of Jews in civil rights organizations was a badge of honor among many Jews, and a source either of appreciation or resentment among Black leaders, depending on their ideological orientation. Nor was the Black-Jewish alliance merely political. In a case that shocked the nation in 1964, two civil rights workers, Michael Schwerner and Andrew Goodman, both Jews, were murdered along with a Black civil rights worker, James Chaney, in Philadelphia, Mississippi, their bodies buried in a dam site and not found for weeks. Jews literally had skin in the game.

The Jewish commitment to civil rights was not, of course, entirely altruistic. A society that limited the rights of Black people also impeded the rights and mobility of Jews. Jews had been routinely prevented from fully participating in American social and business life, and thus had developed Jewish law firms, medical practices, and country clubs. The American Jewish community's sense of self became anchored to its role in the civil rights movement of the 1960s, so much so that when Black Lives Matter—a very different version of the civil rights movement—emerged in 2013 with an animating ideology that borrowed much of the same imagery, but few of the same ethical or policy commitments, many Jews felt duty-bound to support it. While there were always tensions among Blacks and Jews during the civil rights movement, ties began to fray in the mid-1960s. In some cases, whites and Jews were expelled from the leadership ranks of civil rights groups when organizations such as the Student Nonviolent Coordinating Committee (SNCC)—founded in 1960 and one of the primary movers in nonviolent civil rights activism—shifted away from a multiracial coalition to emphasize racial pride and Black self-determination.[21] At that time, a more radical set of Black leaders took center stage, and violent riots erupted, prompting many Jews to move out of the cities and into the suburbs, never to return.

Years later, when Rev. Louis Farrakhan emerged as the charismatic leader of the Nation of Islam, he only exacerbated already simmering tensions between Jews and Blacks. Farrakhan made numerous disparaging remarks about Jews, calling Judaism a "gutter religion." In 2018, he railed against "the Satanic Jew" and told his followers, "When they talk about Farrakhan, call me a hater, you know how they do—call me an anti-Semite. Stop it, I'm anti-termite!"[22] When Farrakhan called for and then led the Million Man March in October of 1995—a rally in Washington, DC, dedicated to fostering self-sufficiency in the Black community and combating negative racial stereotypes in popular culture—Jews implored their Black friends and allies not to attend, and a few—Congressman John Lewis, for instance—took heed. But many prominent Black figures, such as Rosa Parks, Dorothy Height, and Maya Angelou attended the March, and spoke.[23] A willingness to legitimize Farrakhan was an ongoing point of contention between the Jewish and Black communities: a moral chasm in the road to justice. Many Jews could not wrap their heads around the fact that Farrakhan's bigotry didn't instantly disqualify him in the eyes of a community trying to overcome bigotry.

Numerous Black leaders insisted that the Black community, particularly young Black men, needed Farrakhan's leadership to lift them up. Derek Bell, a prominent Black law professor and one of the originators of Critical Race Theory, carped that only Black leaders "are called upon to repudiate and condemn individuals in their groups who do or say outrageous things." Five years after the Million Man March, Farrakhan initiated the Million Family March, once again bringing Black-Jewish relations to a crisis point. In an opinion piece in the *Washington Post,* I decried Black participation in the March, arguing "[S]ome of the most respected African American leaders felt compelled to share the podium with the Nation of Islam leader. Missing...was the public agonizing that we have heard in the past from Black leaders about whether or not to associate with Farrakhan."[24] Support for Farrakhan's work, if not for his explicit antisemitic message, became an ongoing impediment to Black-Jewish relations and dialogue.

When I arrived at the American Jewish Committee (AJC)in the late 90s, a new project was in the works. The Real Estate Apprentice Program (REAP) was an effort to bring Blacks into Washington's commercial real estate industry, where they had long been severely underrepresented.

Since the early 1980s, the AJC Washington regional office had held an active dialogue with Black leaders, meeting for lunch at the AJC office on M Street in DC to discuss social issues—especially, during my time there, Louis Farrakhan's place in the Black community—for about two hours every two weeks. By the late 1990s, some of the Black participants had grown weary of dialogue for dialogue's sake. In one dialogue session, Maudine Cooper—born in Mississippi, the dynamic head of the Greater Washington Urban League and former Chief of Staff to Mayor Marion Barry—bluntly told a Jewish participant, Mike Bush: "You Jews talk a lot but you never do anything."[25] Bush took her words not as an insult but a challenge. A distinguished Harvard Law alum in his late fifties who sported a bow tie and scraggly gray eyebrows, Bush was the Vice President of Real Estate for Giant Foods, the largest supermarket chain in the metropolitan area. (Despite his pedigree and high six figure salary, Bush lived in a modest house in DC with his wife and kids, and took pleasure in making a statement by driving a twenty-year-old blue station wagon with faux wood paneling, that he refused to let die.)

Attending the annual conference in the mid-1990s of the International Council of Shopping Centers—where industry professionals, many real estate developers among them, gathered to discuss market trends—Bush noticed there was only one Black person, out of the nearly one thousand people in attendance: Al Gonsouland, the head of Hechinger, a chain of home improvement centers. Bush got the idea that Jews, who were well represented in real estate, could help diversify the industry. He wanted to recruit aspiring Black men and women into an intensive course in commercial real estate, and—using his extensive industry contacts—identify commercial real estate firms that would provide networking opportunities and guaranteed jobs to top students. I loved the idea and wrote the first grant request, which was funded by DC's Meyer Foundation. Ultimately a joint endeavor of AJC and the Greater Washington Urban League, which was charged with identifying and recruiting participants, REAP was a smashing success. Within a few years, several dozen new Black hires changed the face of the industry. Bush retired from Giant to work on REAP full time, and spun off the project an independent nonprofit operating in cities across the country and abroad. Today there are hundreds of REAP alums in senior positions in real estate, including senior executives at Amazon and the head of real estate of the global furniture company Ikea.

REAP's success kept the local Black-Jewish dialogue alive, involving prominent members from both communities. Longtime Washington Representative of the American Jewish Committee, Hyman Bookbinder—a former civil rights activist and protégé of Eleanor Roosevelt, affectionately known as "Bookie"—was a regular participant. In those days, Washington DC's failing school system loomed large: a reflection of the general failure of the inner city, which had further been laid waste by a raging crack epidemic. Emblematic of the decay of the era was the 1990 arrest of DC Mayor Marion Barry, who served a total of fifteen years in office, in a sting operation for possession of crack cocaine.

The state of DC's public schools was at the top of the agenda of the dialogue. The failure of the school system was documented in excruciating detail by the DC Financial Control Board—which took over the finances of the failing city government—in a report titled "Children in Crisis," which proclaimed that DC Public Schools are "failing...the school system as a whole is in a state of crisis" and "DCPS fails to teach its pupils even the basics of education."[26] The report revealed that DC's kids were relegated to perhaps the poorest-run school system in America. Test scores were catastrophically low. Bathrooms were unusable. Members of the white educated class who hadn't moved to the nearby suburbs for the sake of their functional school systems and their lower crime rates sent their kids almost exclusively to private schools.

In 1999, I joined a local leadership delegation to visit Anacostia High School in the poverty- and crime-stricken Southeast quadrant of the city, where a new, highly promising principal had plans for a turnaround; we were there to learn from her. One of the first things I noticed in the school were the throngs of students sitting along the hallways during instructional time, playing cards and other games. I had never seen anything like that before. "Excuse me," I asked the principal. "Can I ask why these students aren't in class?" She dropped her voice and said somberly, "I have three choices. I can send these students to class, and they'll be disruptive and prevent the other students from learning. I can send them home, and they will get into all kinds of trouble and some will commit crimes." She paused. "Or I can let them play cards in the hallway. Now what would you do?" I had no answer.

In a state of crisis, the schools had been stripped away from DC's elected school board and placed under the authority of an emergency transition Financial Control Board, which Maudine Cooper chaired. A Black participant in the dialogue, an otherwise circumspect school psychologist named Robert, was uncharacteristically animated about the school system where he had worked for the past decade. In one dialogue session, Robert dismissed every idea anyone else raised about how to fix the school system. "That won't work," he said, over and over, shaking his head. Finally, one of the Black participants replied indignantly, "All you do is tell us what won't work. OK then. What will work?" Robert paused and took a long, deep breath. "Some of us think we need to ship out some of the Negroes running the school system and bring in some white folks to run things."

"Why do you say that?" I tentatively asked, breaking the prolonged silence.

"Because it's all cronyism," Robert said. "Most of the Black professional class running things promote each other into positions they aren't qualified for. They've lost the plot. Not enough of them work for these kids. I am going to tell you something shocking. When I started at the school I'm at now, there was a mentally retarded boy named Nelson just roaming the school hallways. I asked the school administration about him. All they could do was acknowledge his existence. He had never even been given psychological testing. Nelson should have been in a special needs program. He should have been accounted for. But he would just show up at school every day and wander around aimlessly and no one did anything." Robert started rubbing his eyes and began to weep. "They did nothing," he added softly.

Bookie, among the most eloquent men I had ever known, stammered, "I just…I just can't believe what I am hearing, I mean I never heard." He shook his head in disbelief or denial—I couldn't tell which—and then he too teared up, removed his spectacles, and wiped his eyes with his white handkerchief. The other Black participants were quiet. Gerald, a Black gay man in his fifties who wore a scarf with an African motif and often defended Farrakhan despite the Minister's homophobic rants, finally muttered, "What a disgrace." Shame showed on the faces of the Black participants. They knew there was no papering over the dysfunction. While they could rightly blame the poor and deteriorating conditions of inner-city Washington on the scourge of past and present racism, they knew that some of the fault lay with the catastrophic failure of Black professionals and leaders, their contemporaries, and even with themselves. They had escaped poverty, they were the lucky ones, and they were now in charge of the systems that were supposed to help the next generation do the same. But although the DC schools had some of the highest per-pupil spending of any school system in the country, at that point not even the school bathrooms worked.

As painful as these encounters could be for all involved, they formed my understanding of "diversity." Project REAP showed me what people could accomplish if they worked together, and became a model for diversifying societal institutions. The model of diversity I knew and valued brought together people of different backgrounds, ethnicities, viewpoints and experiences, often but not always generating a common vision for addressing social challenges. Political scientist Yoscha Mounk calls this model of diversity "cultural patriotism"[27]: enlisting a diverse array of ethnicities and cultures in forming a single nation. By the same token, the Black writer and music critic, Albert Murray, speaks of "antagonistic cooperation,"[28] which he sees in music, literature and race relations. Antagonistic cooperation exists when two persons or groups satisfy a common interest while minor antagonisms of interest are suppressed. I understood diversity as fostering both cultural patriotism and antagonistic cooperation. No one needed to lose for others to win. Society need not be a zero-sum game.

Prejudice Plus Power

Little did I know that there was a model of diversity that was gaining steam in the corporate world, imported from the academic world, that was not based on dialogue among equals, but on fundamentally altered power dynamics that gave voice to society's marginalized. This new model of diversity was based on many of the same intellectual trends I had first observed and experienced in college and then in graduate school, trends that cast American society in an oppressor-versus-oppressed binary, attributing a single explanation for all problems and disparities to that paradigm: systemic racism. This version of diversity would have regarded Robert's assessment of the school system—painful and authentic as it was—as "victim blaming" for holding Black leadership responsible, rather than the all-powerful "White supremacy," for the conditions of schools. This new model would have stifled the kind of discussion that ultimately could allow the school system to fix itself.

In 1998, I was accepted into Leadership Washington, a cohort of business, government and nonprofit leaders who spent a year studying regional challenges and thinking through how to address them. There were about forty of us in the program. Three days were devoted to "Multiculturalism"—what today would be called "Diversity, Equity and Inclusion" or "DEI." I was excited. Multicultural programs were right up my alley. I soon realized, however, this was a totally different approach to diversity. John Butler—the program chair and the head of a Catholic high school in Washington—opened the program, stating that "racism equals prejudice plus power." I had never heard that formulation before. "I think racism is hatred toward other races, and don't think power, whatever that is, has anything to do with it," I told Butler after the meeting. "You can disagree all you want but that's what racism is," he said. I wondered who gave him the final word on the matter. Such insistence on being right was hard for me to stomach; this was a demand for acquiescence.

Then Leadership Washington participants viewed the 1994 film *The Color of Fear*, made by "master diversity trainer" and filmmaker Lee Mun Wah.[29] The film portrayed four men at a weekend retreat talking about racism: one African American, one Latino, one Caucasian, and the filmmaker himself, who was Asian. As far as I could tell, this was a real, unscripted interaction. But from the very beginning, the setup was obvious: the three men of color were all well versed in the language of multiculturalism that would soon become woke jargon. The white guy, however, was apparently a total nitwit. I doubt he'd had a serious conversation in his life, let alone one on issues of race and racism. The three trained diversity hands took turns browbeating the simpleton, who insisted he didn't see color, about how shamefully clueless he was about race. They insisted that his "colorblindness" was a sham, and that it was high time he recognized that his whiteness was a bona fide ethnicity essential to his place in the world. By the time they were done with him, he broke down in tears, finally recognizing his own racism and the role he'd played in perpetuating an unjust society. This display of performative cruelty masquerading as enlightened diversity revolted me.

When the film was over, we broke into groups of eight to discuss what we had just seen. The facilitator of my breakout session, who also happened to be the main organizer of the program, was Howard Ross. You may have heard of Ross; he was organizing the federal DEI training when President Donald Trump issued an executive order to end all CRT-based diversity programs in the federal Government.[30] Ross was the diversity trainer of the stars, having been assigned to, among others, John Rocker, the professional baseball player who had scandalized the sport with his unfiltered bigotry. Ross began our group session with a question: "How did the film make you feel?" After three others shared their deep-seated feelings about our fallen society, some angry and some sad, it was my turn. "I don't know how I feel, but I do know what I think," I stated. "I think it was a terrible film that says nothing about racism."

This frankness did not ingratiate me with the group. I soon found myself in a sequel to the movie itself, and I, the swarthy son of an Iraqi Jewish immigrant who never saw himself as white, was the white guy. An African American pastor of one of the largest congregations in the metropolitan area began to cross-examine me. He asked me if I thought I was a racist. "I try hard not to be," I stated, continuing, "In my teen years, I told tasteless ethnic jokes, but made a very conscious decision not to do it anymore." I said that while I fully recognize the ongoing reality of racism, I didn't think it explained all the problems facing Black people in the inner cities. The pastor, startled by my challenge, bellowed: "What else explains these problems?" I paused and then blurted: "How about young Black school kids who make fun of other Black kids for being too studious? Isn't that a problem too?" This lamentable behavior had been the subject of recent high-profile stories in the press. The pastor glared at me with a mixture of disgust and resignation. But he didn't argue back, signaling, perhaps, that he too was concerned about this phenomenon. A Black female participant sitting next to me quietly nodded in agreement.

Suddenly, I realized that this so-called diversity training was actually a group therapy session for the newly recognized mental illness known as white racism, and I was a patient. The therapist—Howard Ross—was there to push us to acknowledge our own racism, the first step in overcoming any psychological ailment. My non-doctrinaire view on race was a cognitive distortion that could be remedied only through an intense course of diversity therapy. I was not an easy patient. I knew little about the theory behind this brand of diversity training at that time, but I did know this was no way to create a just society or a more collaborative workplace, so I vowed to stay away from this form of social coercion in the future.

Since that time, I have had several interactions, including a very pleasant lunch, with Howard Ross, and I consider him a decent human being. I'm sure he believes his work advances equality. He cheers for the underdog, as do I. Ross now acknowledges that the old style of diversity training was alienating, and that more updated forms—which focus on implicit bias—accord greater respect to people's varied life stories. But I see nothing in today's training, much of it based on the new canon such as Robin DiAngelo's *White Fragility* and Ibram X. Kendi's *How to Be an Antiracist*, that demonstrates any such respect. Moreover, extensive research by Harvard sociology professor Frank Dobbin and others shows that these newer forms are no more effective in achieving workplace inclusion—and are every bit as alienating—as the earlier versions.[31]

I wasn't successful, however, in avoiding further coercive diversity programs. My duties at the American Jewish Committee placed me in several other ideologically saturated "diversity" settings in the ensuing months. At a meeting of the National Conference of Christians and Jews (later renamed the less particularistic National Conference of Community and Justice), I watched a film with other participants on "white privilege," wherein a supposedly wise white woman schooled a group of young people on the concept, which was the first time I encountered this dogmatic formulation of social advantage as well. She insisted that white people enjoyed a kind of societal privilege over non-white people, that was largely invisible to whites. I didn't reject the idea that many whites had advantages that many Blacks lacked, but I recoiled at the all-encompassing nature of the claim. After the film, we were broken into groups, wherein a male psychologist once again asked us to process our feelings about what we had just seen. This ideological and psychologically coercive style of diversity training was clearly gaining ground.

Connecting the Dots

I also began to notice that the same ideology I had seen in diversity training had seeped into progressive political spaces and multi-ethnic coalitions. The standard rhetoric among civil rights groups started to shift away from one seeking opportunity to one asserting oppression. Gone were the days of Martin Luther King Jr.'s color-blind aspirations for the "content of one's character" in favor of a more austere condemnation of the system. In March 2001, I wrote a memo headed "Immigration and American Values," in which I argued that these ideological trends might acculturate a generation of immigrants into a hostile interpretation of American values. I shared the memo with key colleagues at the American Jewish Committee. Several months later, the organization held a special seminar on "Acculturation," where they shared my memo and debated whether the new multiculturalism, as we then called it, would be good or bad for the country. In that memo, I wrote something I could just as well write today:

> In its more radical form, multiculturalism is not merely neutral toward American values, it is openly hostile. Some ideologues go beyond claims of discrimination and make the case that racism is deeply embedded in the American value system itself. In order to dismantle this systemic racism, they assert, a stake must be driven through the "hegemony" of American cultural norms. Echoes of this can, unfortunately, be heard even among some of our partners in the civil rights community. Inasmuch as AJC seeks to preserve a common set of American values, we must contest this effort to eradicate them.... It is my view that we at AJC sometimes become inadvertent accomplices to a flawed multicultural discourse and that we should carefully consider the messages that we give to other minorities, especially new immigrants, in our various encounters. How many times have we been part of an intergroup dialogue or public program when someone in the group waxes on

> about the fundamental racism of American society? How many times have we either lamely nodded our heads or even given such insights our explicit endorsement? We must not, in my view, sacrifice our ideals and values at the altar of intergroup relations.[32]

While I didn't immediately see the connection between the emergent antisemitism after the collapse of the peace process and this ascending model of diversity, I started connecting the dots in 2002, just a year after the antisemitic debacle in Durban, South Africa. In January of 2003, I, once again, wrote an opinion piece in the *Washington Jewish Week* that I could have written today: "Progressive ideologues," I argued, "believe that only people with power can be racists. Under this winner-take-all power paradigm, the formula is 'racism=bigotry + power,' which means that you cannot be racist if you don't have power, and if you do have power, you cannot be a victim. Over time," I continued, "progressives have come to view Jews as a privileged group and part of the American power establishment, and this lends little credence to Jewish claims of racism. So when Jews allege racism by Arabs or Muslims, or African Americans, progressives tend to remain conspicuously silent because, in their view, Jews cannot be victims, and 'powerless' minority groups cannot be guilty of racism."[33]

What I began to see was the convergence of an American version of the post-colonialist ideology I witnessed in Durban, South Africa—a version that has since congealed into woke ideology—and the growth of antisemitism on the Progressive left. The simplistic ideology of "oppressor versus oppressed" fueled antisemitism by linking identity to privilege and—in the minds of some—Jewish identity to "Jewish privilege." Durban was not a one-off, and it was not just a global phenomenon. The American left was being Durbanized, and many American Jews were naively helping it along by acquiescing to the demands of woke ideologues.

CHAPTER 5

THE RISE OF BLACK LIVES MATTER AND THE HYPER-WOKE JEW

All Stories Are Equal

In 2010, I became the Executive Director of the David Project, an organization dedicated to educating and training Jewish college and high school students to advocate for Israel. Early in my tenure, I toured college campuses coast to coast, speaking to dozens of student activists, Jewish campus professionals, and professors, and I came away with a central conclusion: students back then embraced a kind of "soft postmodernism" in which they held that all narratives were equal. They didn't want to be pro-Israeli or pro-Palestinian; they wanted to be pro-Everybody. I asked two Jewish students who attended Ivy League schools, "How would you describe the intellectual climate on your campuses?" One answered, "We don't really have one," and the other responded, "We sort of have one, and it's left-leaning." At Columbia University—a traditional hotbed of political activity—one pro-Israel student leader told me that Israel's Independence Day celebration on campus almost always produced a verbal collision between a handful of outspoken supporters of Israel and a group of Israel's detractors. He said the spectacle alienates even many pro-Israel students, not to mention non-Jewish students, who might otherwise be open to a more sympathetic view of the country. When they saw pro-Israel and anti-Israel students going at it on the campus quad, their instinctive response was "a plague on both your houses."

I realized that the average student wasn't much interested in debating competing claims—they were largely conflict-averse—about who is right or wrong. They believed everyone and every group had its own story, and no story was better than any other. I thought this "everyone is right" worldview was astoundingly shallow. My friend Rabbi Jeffrey Salkin told me that he tells his high school students who express similar sentiments: "Don't be so open-minded that everything falls out." My private assessment of the "everyone is right" worldview was that everything had indeed fallen out of these very open-minded students, but I also understood that my job was not to make them better critical thinkers but to figure out how to influence their views on Israel and the Israeli-Palestinian conflict. My job was to train Jewish student leaders in the words of an Israeli advertisement promoting safer driving: "Don't be right, be smart," a phrase we used a lot with Jewish student leaders.

In the winter of 2012, the David Project took a group of non-Jewish student leaders to Israel—student body presidents, newspaper editors, progressive leaders and activists, and others—along with their Jewish student counterparts, to understand the array of narratives that make up the Israeli people. We wanted the students to see Israel and Israelis—secular and religious, peaceniks and settlers, Jews and Arabs—in all their glorious complexity. One of our first meetings on the trip was at the YMCA in Jerusalem, a Byzantine-style stone complex with elegant arches, domes, and an iconic observation tower overlooking Jerusalem's old and new cities. There we met the charismatic, well-dressed Israeli Arab CEO of the YMCA, Forsan Hussein. In addition to his native Arabic, Hussein spoke fluent Hebrew and English, having attained degrees from Brandeis, Johns Hopkins, and Harvard Business School.[34] Hussein was a master of the narrative. He mesmerized the visiting students with stories of his childhood in a village in Galilee in the northern part of Israel, where he had had no experience of Jews, and believed what he was taught: that Jews had horns. Then, at age fifteen, when he finally met Jewish youth from the nearby moshav (Israeli farming community), he discovered that they, in turn, grew up believing "Palestinians had tails." I rolled my eyes: Hussein was embroidering: in fact, Israeli Arabs and Jews grew up together, knowing their differences and similarities from birth, so no way did Hussein ever actually believe any of that nonsense. But the students hung on his every word.

The following day, the same set of students met the very cerebral Palestinian journalist Khaled Abu Toameh, known for his independent reporting and for bucking the Palestinian party line. A female student excitedly asked him what he thought about Forsan Hussein's experience growing up thinking Jews had horns. Toameh responded, "I think that's total BS," and went on to the next question. The student looked disappointed at the dismissal. Later that evening, I debriefed with the students about the various meetings. The same female student asked me "Why did Khaled Abu Toameh discount the narrative of Forsan Hussein?" I took a deep breath and answered: "Because Forsan Hussein's story was total bullshit. There's no way that Forsan grew up thinking that Jews had horns, because he undoubtedly interacted with many Jews all his life, and there's no way Israeli Jews thought Palestinians had tails—they grew up around Israeli Arabs!" Later that evening, one of the campus professionals, Jason, approached me and reported: "You should know that some of the students are smack-talking you because you discredited Forsan Hussein." I realized then I had committed the cardinal sin in the eyes of that generation of students: I discounted another's narrative. I vowed not to do it again.

I learned during the lead-up to the Israel trip that one of our campus professionals had recruited Tina, the head of the African American Student Union and a member of student government at a California college, who had supported Boycott, Divestment, and Sanctions (BDS) against Israel. Groups like the David Project were created to oppose BDS on campus, and taking a known BDS activist on a fully funded trip to Israel might generate a firestorm in the Jewish community. Not wanting to burn bridges to her campus, we decided to chance it and bring Tina on the mission. Later, I heard from our campus professionals that after seeing Israel, warts and all, and hearing the stories of so many Israelis firsthand, Tina had a change of heart. She came to appreciate that the conflict with the Palestinians was far more complicated than she was led to believe. As we prepared to sit down for dinner one evening, Tina walked up to me and asked if she could have a word. "Of course," I said. "You may be aware that I voted to support the BDS resolution in student government," she said. "I am," I answered. "After being in Israel for the past week, I've come to realize that vote was a mistake," she choked up. She put her head down, no longer looking me in the eye. "I'm asking for your forgiveness," she stated softly. "Tina, you don't have to apologize for your views. I'm just grateful you are open-minded enough to rethink your perspectives in light of what you've seen." So our multiple-narrative approach to Israel advocacy did open up hearts and minds. It was working.

Having witnessed firsthand the power of telling stories, the team at the David Project decided to bring in a consultant with expertise in interpersonal storytelling, to train the staff to teach Jewish student activists how best to talk to different types of students—be they members of environmental, women's, LGBT rights, Black, Hispanic, or Asian organizations. During the training, one of our campus professionals, Jordana, a sometimes-quarrelsome young woman from New Jersey in her mid-twenties, interrupted the session: "I really think we need to take a moment before we discuss how we are going to message to marginalized communities, and acknowledge our own privilege." Everyone fell silent. "Jordana," I said, "we are not going to do that. This is a training session on how to talk to different segments of the population." "I know!" she insisted, "That's exactly why we need to acknowledge our privilege. By trying to influence marginalized people, we are engaging in a specific kind of power dynamics, and we shouldn't really do this work unless we gain their approval and understand our own role in these power dynamics."

I grew impatient. I didn't mind a young staff person challenging me—far from it. I worked hard to create a culture in which younger staff members felt free to challenge their supervisors, including me. But her incessant entreaties made it impossible to conduct our training. She simply refused to let us continue. Later that day, I overheard some of the younger staff members discussing the incident. "We do really need to acknowledge our privilege," stated one. This was the first of numerous incidents in which young Progressive staff members insisted that their views on power and privilege, undoubtedly heartfelt, gave them license to disrupt workplace activities.

A New Campus Vibe

When school came back to session in the Fall of 2014, the David Project team immediately noticed the campus climate had changed. Our campus professionals reported that many of the non-Jewish students they were cultivating had become standoffish and even hostile. Jewish students shared their anxieties with us about the worsening campus climate toward Israel. Jason, a campus professional, came to see me. "Bad news," he said. "Tina is supporting BDS again on her campus." I felt like someone had punched me in the gut. Hadn't our relational story-telling method worked? I didn't yet understand the shift in ideological attitudes taking place beneath the surface.

On August 10, 2014, in Ferguson, Missouri, Michael Brown was shot and killed by police officer Darren Wilson.[35] Mass unrest followed, sparking a national debate about the relationship between law enforcement and the Black community, the "militarization" of the police, and use-of-force laws in states across the country. Black Lives Matter, born in the wake of the Trayvon Martin killing two years earlier, was now a force to be reckoned with. The unrest gained steam that November when a grand jury did not indict Officer Wilson. With Black students at the forefront, Brown's death radicalized campus politics practically overnight. Black Lives Matter had no "everyone is right" category in its narrative—the white-dominated state oppressed Black people, period. Social psychologist Jonathan Haidt also speaks of the trends in social media in the preceding years that conspired to shift the discourse. "That really came to fruition in 2014," he told Andrew Sullivan.[36] "We started getting craziness on both sides of the Atlantic. That's when Gamergate starts, which is the first big mob attack public thing. That's when weird stuff starts happening on campus. That's when Greg Lukianoff [President of the Foundation for Individual Rights and Expression, then a campus free speech organization] comes to talk to me and say, "Jon, weird stuff is happening. It wasn't there in 2012." Gone was the soft postmodernism of multiple narratives, replaced by a hard postmodernism of binary power structures, that expressed in no uncertain terms who had power and who was powerless, who was oppressed and who was doing the oppressing.

Intersectionality Fever

In the fall of 2015, after I had left the David Project to start my own consulting business, I was invited by the Israel on Campus Coalition of Greater Washington to conduct a training seminar on Israel advocacy for Jewish student leaders. I shared my observation that varied Progressive student groups were beginning to connect their causes. Each of them now featured a fixed sense of oppressor and oppressed. Feminist, Black, and LGBT activists were expressing solidarity with the Palestinians. During the Black Lives Matter protests in Ferguson, signs reading "From Ferguson to Palestine" began to appear. Tweets from Palestinian activists stating "it is always the oppressed standing with the oppressed" were retweeted hundreds of thousands of times. A video produced by BLM activists likening the Black lives cause to the Palestinian cause went viral. "That's called intersectionality," a Georgetown University student named Max stated matter-of-factly. "And it really scares me, because there doesn't seem to be anything we can do or say to influence the thinking of the students who buy into it." I vaguely remembered studying "intersectionality" in graduate school: this term was coined by Kimberle Crenshaw in 1989, to describe a framework for understanding how aspects of a person's social and political identities combine to create different modes of discrimination and privilege.[37] It was originally a legal framework that was meant to address a loophole in the law that let companies off the hook for discriminating against Black women, who were not a distinct protected class. But it soon became much more. Intersectionality holds that a person who is, for example, both Black and female experiences greater disadvantage than if she belonged to just one or the other oppressed group—if she were just Black or just female. By the same token, a person who is both white and male experiences added privilege than if he fit just one of those identity categories. While intersectionality is supposedly about the relationship of identity to power, many of the activists used the term to describe their affinity and solidarity with other causes. An LGBT rights organization, for example, might, in the name of intersectionality, express solidarity with an indigenous rights organization. Like so many other social justice concepts, intersectionality has some utility in describing social dynamics, but activists have transformed a simple heuristic into a grand axiom and then into an article of faith.

In January of 2016, I became President and CEO of the Jewish Council for Public Affairs (JCPA), the then seventy-year-old Jewish advocacy and community relations umbrella for the American Jewish community. On my first day on the job, the Jewish Telegraphic Agency (JTA) published an opinion piece I wrote, "The Anti-Israel Trend You've Never Heard Of," in which I argued that intersectionality was a real and present danger to the Jewish community. "If a group sees itself as oppressed," I wrote, "it will see Israel as part of the dominant power structure doing the oppressing and Palestinians as fellow victims. That oppressed group will be susceptible to joining forces with the BDS movement." I concluded: "The growing acceptance of intersectionality arguably poses the most significant community relations challenge of our time. Ultimately, how popular—and how threatening—intersectionality becomes depends on the degree to which the far left, constituting about 10 percent of society, is successful in inculcating its black-and-white worldview, simplistic perspectives, and resentment toward those perceived as powerful with the mainstream left."[38] Regrettably, the dangers I warned about have come to pass: the far left has succeeded in inculcating its worldview throughout an ever-widening swath of the mainstream left.

My article caught the attention of many in the Jewish community and prompted the publication of several opinion pieces rebuking me for my views. The ideological left of the Jewish community, which held intersectionality as a cornerstone of their progressive politics, was enraged. In *New Voices*, Chloe Sobel responded, "Intersectionality is valuable not because it can make Israel look better. It's valuable because it can make Israel *be* better.... Intersectionality encourages progressives who care about social justice in the United States to care about social justice in Israel."[39] A former colleague of mine, Jody—who worked for a progressive Jewish advocacy organization—saw my use of the term as an insult to her work that, she said, was deeply intersectional. Many others, however, told me that they had never heard of "intersectionality," and that they saw the danger in the concept of fueling disdain for Israel.

Several of my new colleagues told me that my article might compromise the Jewish community's ability to engage the Progressive left on issues of concern, and urged me to recant. The Director of the Jewish Community Relations Council of San Francisco, Abby Porth, said that her young staff were experts on intersectionality, and we should ask them to educate other Jewish advocates across the country. Every noxious ideological fad the larger American Jewish community faced seemed to originate in the politically charged San Francisco Bay Area, and the staff at Jewish organizations there often had more experience in addressing them than the rest of the country, so we organized a webinar for the Jewish advocacy community called "Grappling with Intersectionality."

While I didn't say so explicitly, I came to believe that the mainstream Jewish community needed to find a way to include the Jewish narrative in the intersectional matrix—to complicate it—so that Jews and Israel were not viewed as the perennial oppressors and Palestinians the perennial victims. Jews needed to be viewed as one of the oppressed groups. Concerned about the growing backlash to my article, I used the opportunity of the webinar to soften my stance on the topic, stating "I still have much to learn" and that "intersectionality is a complex, interesting, and nuanced phenomenon that we need to understand, not just from the perspective of the pro-Israel community, but from its own perspective as well." During the ensuing panel discussion, Joe, a young LGBT staff member of the Jewish Community Relations Council of San Francisco, stated flatly, "We are all intersectional. We all bring our identities into the spaces in which we operate.... We are also shaped by our own privileges. As Jewish community relations professionals, it's important to know what our blind spots are as we engage in our work." Joe wasn't providing direction on how to navigate the current ideological landscape; he was inculcating the audience in the ideology itself.[40]

A few weeks later, still making amends, the JCPA held a panel discussion on intersectionality at our national conference in Cleveland, Ohio, with Ilana Kaufman, a dynamic Black-Jewish woman who worked in the Eastern Bay area, and Marla Brettschneider, a Professor of Women's Studies at the University of New Hampshire. Brettschneider had recently written a book about Jewish women in intersectional feminism. In preparation for the session, I asked Kaufman, "What should we do if people in the audience disagree with the intersectional framework?" She paused, then said, "We should bring those people along." Brettschneider nodded in enthusiastic agreement. I was speechless; neither woman would tolerate any questioning of her preferred ideological framework. What could I say to a speaker who refuses to allow disagreement in a discussion?

Locked in the Blind Reflex

Such ideological displays also kept popping up in the internal workings of my organization. As in many organizations, relations between JCPA managers and employees could be tense. I was a big fan of the book *Seeing Systems: Unlocking the Mysteries of Organizational Life*, by Barry Oshry, which exposes common organizational dynamics. Oshry observes, "In the Dance of Blind Reflex, Top (leader-manager) becomes increasingly responsible for the organization, classroom, department, meeting, team, family, nation—while Bottom becomes decreasingly responsible.... And these shifts happen without awareness or choice by either Top or Bottom. Top falls into burden—carrying the load of the problem, feeling like he or she is letting the system down, worrying—while Bottom falls into oppression—holding Top responsible for the failure, feeling like a blameless sufferer because of Top's inadequacy."[41] In other words, a common pattern in organizations is for managers and direct reports to become locked in a dance, whereby managers take on too much of the burden of the organization's work, and direct reports are left with little control over their work. They both complain about it.

I decided to address the problem of the dance of the blind reflex in my organization, at an offsite retreat in the Spring of 2016. I had team members read an extended version of Oshry's example, complete with dialogue, to inspire managers to relinquish some of their control so that their employees had more freedom in their jobs. It did not go as planned. Three young staffers, whom this exercise was meant to benefit, vociferously objected. "This is victim-blaming," one young woman insisted. I realized that these staffers were looking at an organizational problem through a binary social justice lens in which the powerful are always wrong and the powerless are always right. The blind reflex exercise, in their view, was not a call for their bosses to share power as I intended, but rather an assault on their worldview in which the oppressor class—the bosses of society—cause all social ills. The discussion got so heated that eventually I abandoned the whole exercise and, with it, a framework that was meant to give younger employees more control over their work; I allowed these young staffers to have their way. In retrospect, I now see how organizations like the ACLU, through repeated capitulation, can be captured by young ideologues. They repeatedly complain, and the organization folds.

But I later realized that these young staffers may have had a point in one respect: The Dance of the Blind Reflex was indeed an apt metaphor for what was happening in society at large, not just in organizational life. In American society, the "Tops" and "Bottoms" do in fact conspire to deprive the Bottoms of agency. Woke ideologues claim to see the system not as a dance, but rather as a fully scripted play wherein the Bottoms have little if any agency. The ideologues paradoxically play out their role as Tops, discouraging the Bottoms from exercising agency. Oshry's solution to the problem was to generate greater awareness of system dynamics so that the dancers—Top and Bottom—could end this toxic dance. At the societal level, woke ideologues and policy-makers conspire to keep it going.

Shed your Whiteness

In the Fall of 2016, when a group of Black Jews organized a meeting with Black Lives Matter activists in New York, I jumped at the chance to join it. I was initially denied entry, because the Black Jewish activists who organized the meeting viewed the intersectionality article I had written as an assault on their basic oppressed-versus-oppressor narrative. But after lengthy discussions with Abby Levine of the Jewish Social Justice Roundtable, a proxy for one of the organizers—discussions in which I was told I needed to "do the work"—I grudgingly issued a *mea culpa* as the price of admission, and was finally allowed in. In August 2016, an offshoot of the loosely knit BLM movement, the Movement for Black Lives (M4BL), issued a platform that, among other things, denounced Israel for committing genocide against Palestinians. Jewish leaders accused the platform's authors of antisemitism. Jeremy Burton, the progressive director of the Boston Jewish Community Relations Council, issued a statement rejecting "participation in any coalition that seeks to isolate and demonize Israel singularly amongst the nations of the world" and stated that we "dissociate ourselves from the Black Lives Matter platform and those BLM organizations that embrace it." Faced with relentless criticism, he later recanted, stating "I've lost count of the number of times during a meeting with a group of people, public or private, 2016 and what happened comes up," Burton said. "I've come to accept that the work of *teshuvah* (making amends) is ongoing and talking about the damage created by mistakes is necessary."[42] BLM activists countered Jewish criticism by accusing Jewish leaders of "decentering" the Black experience and distracting attention from their claims—a charge I would hear repeatedly and will discuss in later chapters. Even as we reeled in response to the rising tensions, many Jewish leaders were intensely curious. Who were these unnamed Black Lives Matter activists? Could we win them over and make common cause?

The Jewish leaders who attended the meeting were told in advance that we were expected to show up and listen, to be seen and not heard. We would have time afterward to ask questions in small groups, but we were not allowed to challenge anything we heard during the main discussion. They were authentic voices of the marginalized, and we were merely there to behold their words.

That evening saw many firsts. For the first time, I heard Black Jews say white Jews had benefited from white supremacy and needed to "shed your whiteness," the cultural identity that afforded whites advantage. White Jews, they told us, had taken full advantage of white privilege and their proximity to the white power structure. I later came to understand that—like other privileged ethnicities, such as Asian Americans—many Jews were "white adjacent." We were expected to acknowledge our complicity in white supremacy. Our role moving forward, we were told, was to acknowledge our own guilt, and "make space" for and "lift up" Black voices. This was not your father or mother's civil rights movement, and it was no dialogue; I doubt even the organizers would have described it as such. We were there to learn that we were complicit in the oppression of Black people in America and of Black Jews, and that we "had work to do" on ourselves and in the larger society.

At the end of the meeting, one of the organizers drew the Black participants into a circle. She preached, "I was blind but now I am Woke."

The participants repeated the chant and loudly proclaimed AMEN. I have always been moved by the spiritual fervor of the Black church. Through gospels, hymns, and professions of faith, churchgoers experience a deep, authentic connection to the divine spirit that I could not access. But seeing that same fervor arise during what I understood as a political program confused me, until I realized that the call to be woke was, in fact, a profession of faith. To be woke was to see the light of racial domination and all that it entailed. I felt like I was witnessing a religious revival in service of a new spiritual, political and social movement.[43]

Woke ideology sees itself not merely as a social movement to end racism but as a complete worldview that supersedes the existing white supremacist order. The ideology has its own internal logic, its own vocabulary, its own history, philosophy, and conception of morality and law. And, like all religions, woke ideology embodies a dogma that rebukes all challenges.

From what I saw, woke ideology insists that only Black people have the right to enunciate Black experiences and claims against society, and that everyone else must abide by their pronouncements. To get in the good graces of the Black activists, it seemed, everyone would have to adopt these pieties. It turns out that many Progressives were eager to be in their good graces.

Can we Engage?

Fresh from the experience in New York, I wrote an opinion piece in the New York *Jewish Week* in October 2016, where I argued, "The Jewish community, which prides itself on its historic commitment to social justice, has every reason to join the cause of helping America live up to its own ideals of equality. And if the community wants to have any influence on how today's civil rights activists view Jews and Jewish issues, it must show up to the planning meetings, press conferences and protests." But, I cautioned, "it will not be easy integrating the Jewish community into civil rights coalitions, some of which hold very different political sensibilities. Young activists routinely invoke phrases like "white supremacy" to describe America's prevailing power structure, and this may sound extreme to many mainstream Jews. Rather than feeling obliged to use these terms, however, the Jewish community can develop its own social justice vocabulary and come to the table in its own voice."[44] Unfortunately, the mainstream Jewish community never was allowed to come to the table "in its own voice," or never bothered to try. Woke ideology prescribes only one voice and thus forces two choices: adopt the ideology or be part of the problem.

CHAPTER 6

WHEN EVERYONE LOST THEIR MINDS

It's the Harm

The rise of woke ideology became highly personal when I got an unexpected call in May 2019 from my son's school principal: she had suspended my son for the remainder of his eighth-grade year—three and a half weeks—for appearing in the background of a video made by another boy, who held a gun—not a real gun, a disabled airsoft gun that shoots plastic pellets. My son's school had investigated and found that, in addition to the other boy's video, my son had taken a selfie of the other kid holding him in a headlock and pointing the fake gun at my son's head. My son then shared his selfie, without comment, with 13 friends on Snapchat. The boys did all of this in my basement, not on school premises.

"This is very, very serious," the principal intoned. I didn't think it was serious at all. I thought the length of the suspension was brutishly draconian. An unloaded airsoft gun is not one step away from an AK-47. A kid with poor enough judgment to pose with an airsoft gun is not one step away from shooting up his school with a real gun; he is one step away from being an adolescent knucklehead who needs, perhaps, a couple days of intense reflection. When I went to the principal's office to plead for leniency, she told me my son's photo had upset students who already had anxiety issues. "It's the harm, not the intent, that matters," she stated a matter-of-factly.

I had already run into this latest woke moral platitude about harm vs. intent. In their 2018 book *The Coddling of the American Mind*, Jonathan Haidt and Greg Lukianoff explain, "Some activists say that bigotry is only about impact, as they define impact. Intent is not even necessary. If a member of an identity group feels offended or oppressed by the action of another person, then…that other person is guilty of an act of bigotry."[45]

The world saw this woke, harm-based morality on full display when Don McNeil, the highly respected *New York Times* science reporter, resigned from the paper early in 2021. One of McNeil's supposed sins occurred in 2019 when he quoted someone using the N-word while on an official *Times* trip with high school students in Peru. He was asked by a student whether he thought a classmate should have been suspended for a video she had made as a 12-year-old in which she used the N-word. McNeil asked the student if her classmate called someone else the N-word—and stated the term—or whether she was quoting someone. In January 2021, after an internal investigation, McNeil was subjected to undisclosed disciplinary action but ultimately allowed to keep his job after the executive editor of the *Times* determined that "his intentions [did not appear to be] hateful or malicious."[46]

After McNeil's partial exoneration, 150 *Times* staffers wrote to the publisher, urging that the newspaper take further action: "Our harassment training makes clear that what matters is how an act makes a victim feel; Mr. McNeil's victims weren't shy about decrying his conduct on the trip. We, his colleagues, feel disrespected by his actions. The company has a responsibility to take those feelings seriously."[47] So the *Times* forced McNeil out, further establishing an absurd "moral" principle that only invited others to cancel their colleagues for speech they didn't like, and school principals to suspend kids for lengthy periods of time for making other kids and perhaps their overbearing parents feel a bit nervous.

'White Intellectualism'

In the spring of 2020, more woke ideology alarm bells went off in my head when Abby Levine of the Jewish Social Justice Roundtable asked my organization, the Jewish Council for Public Affairs, to sign a petition accusing two respected Jewish scholars, Ira Sheskin and Arnold Dashevsky, of engaging in racism for an article the two wrote, which stated there were fewer Jews of color than a recent study indicated. I was friendly with Sheskin, a social scientist living in South Florida, and knew him to be anything but a racist. He and Dashevsky cited research—including a 2013 Pew study, the most comprehensive data set to date—that indicated that the actual number of American Jews of color was about 6 percent, instead of the 12–15 percent claimed in the previous study.[48] An outcry immediately erupted: progressive groups launched a petition that garnered more than 2,500 signatures, decrying the supposed sins of the authors. Woke critics attacked Sheskin and Dashevsky, claiming their findings disempowered and erased Jews of color. Leaders of the Reform Movement accused the authors of "white intellectualism" and erasure.[49]

I had never heard Jewish leaders use the term "intellectualism" as a pejorative, but these critics argued that the social scientists' article should never have been published. One would think from reading these indictments that Sheskin and Dashevsky had issued a broadside against Jews of color. Nothing could be further from the truth. Rather, they found that "Responsible planning by the American Jewish community demands recognition that not all Jews are of Eastern Europe and Ashkenazi origin, and future research on American Jews needs to be sensitive to discerning Jews of Color." I was shocked at the attacks on these two scholars for the crime of doing social science research, and I told Abby Levine that JCPA would not sign the petition. I felt bad for Sheskin and called him up to express my regret. But given the prominence of the signatories of the petition, several of whose organizations were members of my organization, I didn't feel I could publicly defend the two scholars without causing major fallout. In 2021, a year after the cancellation campaign against Sheskin and Dashevsky, out came a new Pew Study, eight years after the first, which indicated that Jews of color now make up 8 percent of the American Jewish community.[50] I interviewed Sheskin—the first time he spoke on the record since the fiasco. He explained, "The 8 percent (cited in the Pew study) is about what we would expect given the 6 percent seven years ago." He and Dashevsky were vindicated. But no one ever apologized to them for impugning their work and damaging their reputations.

Post-Floyd Blowback

I didn't think the ideological environment could get any worse. A week later, however, all hell broke loose when George Floyd, a forty-six-year-old Black man, was murdered by Derek Chauven, a forty-four-year-old white Minneapolis police officer. When I first saw reports of the offense on social media referring to video footage recorded by an onlooker's smartphone and several security cameras, I didn't have the heart to watch Chauvin keep his knee on Floyd's neck, pinned to the ground for several minutes, as life drained from his body. The spectacle sickened me, and I braced for yet another round of public reactions to the death of an unarmed Black man at the hands of a white police officer. What I wasn't prepared for was how unhinged everyone became in the so-called "reckoning" about race that followed.

A week after the murder, *eJewish Philanthropy* published an innocuous opinion piece I had submitted weeks earlier, in which I wondered whether Jewish organizations still needed physical office spaces, given the ease with which people worked from home during the pandemic. "It's high time we ask ourselves whether we could do without physical office space or come to a new understanding of how often our staffs need to be together in person," I said. In the comments, a Reconstructionist rabbi accused me of acting out of "privilege" for not acknowledging that some people might lack personal space to work from home. "Home office privilege," I thought to myself. "Now that's a new one."[51] A highly influential professional leader chimed in on Facebook: "Having spaces at home to work is a luxury not a lot of people have. Workspaces out of the home are a psychological necessity for a lot of people." I responded, "There's an equally compelling case for not requiring people to spend hours a day in transit." Another high-profile Jewish professional known for his progressive politics warned me via text: "You wouldn't want people to think that you've lost track of your leadership responsibilities during times of strife and during COVID"—delivering what philosopher Oliver Traldi once called a "rhexortation"[52]—a rhetorical exhortation not to express a certain "problematic" point of view. These responses to my views on office space were not critiques of my slant on the matter. A critique would be "I disagree with you because…." These were rebukes. And rebukes are designed to shut people down. "Fine," I thought to myself. "Keep your fucking corner offices with the big windows and city views."

A colleague of mine who worked for a Jewish organization told me of the blowback he experienced in the aftermath of the George Floyd killing: "We issued a very strong public statement condemning the George Floyd murder. We said all the right things and specifically cited the role of systemic racism. But I've been getting incredible flack because we didn't involve a Jew of color in the drafting of the statement." "Apparently," I responded, "Jewish organizations are no longer allowed to even say all the right things without a Jew of color helping them say them." In this new racial reckoning, white people lacked legitimacy to speak on matters of race.

At an organization board meeting held a few weeks after Floyd's death, I gave my President's Report, laying out the steps we were prepared to take in the fight for racial justice: We would strengthen ties to important Black partners such as the NAACP, we would expand our work in criminal justice and police reform, and we would recruit and empower Jews of color in our leadership ranks. "But," I stated, choosing my words carefully, fully aware of the impending woke onrush, "we must also be mindful not to stifle alternative points of view. Some who speak in the name of racial justice want to shut down discussion on important topics, and it's vital that we stand up for our values of open discourse. We should also keep in mind that America, for all its faults, is a country that has provided unparalleled equality and prosperity to millions." Strangely, not one Board member responded. "No one wants to take a chance that they'll be called out by someone else on the Board," one Board member told me after the meeting. "Marcy told me she agrees with you but just doesn't need the headache."

Macro and Micro-Cancellations

So it wasn't any one brazen act of cancellation aimed at a well-respected news reporter, a prominent data scientist, or a beloved poet that convinced me that woke ideology was out of control, wreaking havoc. I was alerted by my own growing sense of danger, the certainty that I and others could no longer safely express a discordant viewpoint. The high-profile cases of cancellation could easily eclipse the everyday reproach that stifles people and helps set the culture. High-profile cancellation campaigns like those targeting J.K. Rowling or Dave Chappelle, instructive though they are, allow cancel culture deniers to claim that cancellation is rare when, in fact, it's common. Cancellation became a regular feature of social discourse. It occurs in tiny increments, in "micro-cancellations"—subtle, everyday tactics that shut people down. Micro-cancellations short-circuit authentic self-expression and result in fear-invoked self-censorship. More so than the high profile acts we hear about on the Bill Maher show, micro-cancellations—the subtle rebukes, the sneering rhetoric, the pervasive snark, the critiques not of argument but of character—generate the fetid "culture" in "cancel culture."

How did all of this censoriousness come about? In the highly emotional moment following the Floyd murder, those already advocating for a racial reckoning aggressively intervened in societal institutions. Longstanding demands for "action" were finally met. Commitments were made to do things differently. The Equity Review was set into motion. The DEI program that the CEO never wanted was placed on the calendar. The anti-racist audit was conducted. New people were hired to make sure that the organization lived up to its myriad commitments, and people in power deferred to these voices on matters of diversity. Shrill voices on social media were now unencumbered. Demands that people were fired led to people actually getting fired without so much as a hearing. This all provided a permission structure for a kind of incessant bullying by progressive activists.

In July of 2020, more than 150 public intellectuals, writers, and activists signed "A Letter on Justice and Open Debate," which appeared in *Harper's Magazine*, stating, "Our cultural institutions are facing a moment of trial. Powerful protests for racial and social justice are leading to overdue demands for police reform, along with wider calls for greater equality and inclusion across our society, not least in higher education, journalism, philanthropy, and the arts. But this needed reckoning has also intensified a new set of moral attitudes and political commitments that tend to weaken our norms of open debate and toleration of differences in favor of ideological conformity. As we applaud the first development, we also raise our voices against the second."[53] Reading this letter, I felt a combination of gratitude and relief—I was not alone. The letter captured precisely what I was thinking and feeling, and I was glad to be in such good company amid omnipresent censoriousness.

In the American Jewish community, where norms of civility seemed still to reign, micro-cancellations tended to be subtle enough not to violate these norms explicitly, but were commanding enough to send the unmistakable message that everyone should toe the woke party line. One Jewish advocacy professional from a conservative Southern town posed a question on a professional listserv: "What does it say when none of you are able to send me any documented statements from BLM activists against anti-Semitism or BDS [Boycott, Divestment, and Sanctions against Israel]?... I am fully supportive of the Jewish community's engagement with the current civil rights challenge of our time. At the same time, we can't keep sweeping the anti-Semitism under the rug and saying there are BLM leaders and activists who are standing up against anti-Semitism and for Israel if in reality there aren't."

This email prompted a reprimand from one of the more progressive professionals in our network, who stated emphatically "You talk about this (BLM) as 'their' movement, in contrast to 'our' movement—*our* movement being the fight against antisemitism...and *their* movement being the fight for racial equity. We need to shift this language. The fight for racial equity is a Jewish cause if for no other reason than that there are Black Jews who face discrimination in this country for being Black."[54] This response chided the writer's perceived moral failure to see the Black Lives Matter cause as her own. The person responding didn't even address the original writer's concern—that the BLM movement had been silent, or worse, on antisemitism. And no one, me included, dared to defend the writer against the reprimand, for fear that we too would get called on the carpet.

Of course, not all the rebuking was subtle. In the summer of 2020, I organized a meeting on racial justice with leaders in the Jewish community. Present in the meetings was a former colleague—let's call him Jeremy—who'd unknowingly stepped on a landmine while inquiring about the number of Jews of color in the United States. When Jeremy innocently asked about the actual data, one of the higher-status Jewish leaders in his group angrily called him out. "We are not discussing this," he insisted, suggesting that any disagreement about the numbers of Jews of color was beyond the pale. No one—including me, I am ashamed to say—came to his defense. Later that week, I heard from another meeting participant that several participants in the meeting had accused Jeremy of making "inappropriate" and "racist" remarks—by which they meant his reference to the numbers of Jews of color. I continued to stay mute, fearing that speaking up would compromise my position in the group. I called up Jeremy later that day—by then a familiar ritual. "Sorry you had to go through that," I said. But we both knew that being "sorry" doesn't mean much if you don't say anything publicly.

How not to Address Social Problems

The deluge of woke ideology not only exacerbated internal tensions, but it also impaired the Jewish community's ability to engage in policy advocacy designed to fix the broken system. In the fall after the Floyd killing, the JCPA pulled together a Zoom meeting of a coalition called Jews for Criminal Justice Reform, which included top Jewish criminal justice activists from around the country and focused on mobilizing Jews in the fight for reform. After an inspiring talk by Paul Fishman—a former federal attorney from New Jersey—on the need to end mass incarceration, we broke up into smaller groups to discuss next steps. A lawyer named Jared, the group facilitator for the breakout session I was in, asked, "What do you all think our criminal justice reform priorities ought to be?" Ariella, a young professional staffer from a Jewish civil rights organization, interjected, "Before we talk about strategy, there's a lot of internal work we have to do in the Jewish community. We need to recognize our complicity in white supremacy and ensure we have Black Jews at the forefront of these efforts." Zachary, a criminal justice advocate in his forties who worked for the State, replied on cue, "I agree that it's important to center Black voices."

"Here we go again," I thought to myself, "a young staff person holding our work hostage until we recite the prescribed litany of woke pieties." What, pray tell, did Ariella think all this self-reflection would do to help Black people get out of jail for low-level drug charges, or to ensure that time in prison didn't permanently disenfranchise them from society? I suspect she didn't have a clue. Our breakout session never discussed a single criminal justice reform measure. We just sang along with the choir or held our tongues. According to Ryan Grim, in an extensive account in *The Intercept* in June 2022, this penchant to turn inward to reflect on woke platitudes has brought progressive policy advocacy to a standstill. Grim wrote:

> So much energy has been devoted to the internal strife and internal bullshit that it's had a real impact on the ability for groups to deliver," said one organization leader who departed his position. "It's been huge, particularly over the last year and a half or so, the ability for groups to focus on their mission, whether it's reproductive justice, or jobs, or fighting climate change.[55]

Grim's account is exactly what I observed in the progressive Jewish world—young woke employees taking over and sidetracking the organization's work.

Woke discourse also hurts policy advocacy work by cutting out political moderates who could help pass legislation. In 2018, the JCPA hired Roy, a dynamic, formerly incarcerated Black man, to direct and inspire action on criminal justice reform. Roy often quoted Michelle Alexander, author of the celebrated book *The New Jim Crow*: "Mass incarceration is designed to warehouse a population deemed disposable."[56] In this view, mass incarceration is not the accidental outgrowth of bad policy from the crime scare of the early 1990s, but an intentional effort to oppress and "warehouse" Black people. Like Alexander herself, Roy presented these perspectives on the justice system as facts, leaving little room for disagreement and alienating political moderates who might otherwise have been involved in criminal justice reform. A few people asked me whether Roy could tone it down, pointing out that moderates may criticize the justice system and agree that it needs reform, but they aren't likely to go along with shrill, conspiratorial rhetoric. By then, however, Roy's approach was well entrenched.

On a visit to Nashville in the fall of 2000, I gave a presentation to a local criminal justice coalition. I asked point blank: "Can people who agree that there are major problems with the criminal justice system but disagree that America is a white supremacist country have a place at the coalition table?" Much to my surprise, the answer from the activists was a resounding NO. Every single activist considered such a profession of belief *de rigueur*. If the primary goal of the coalition was indeed reforming the system, then coalition members should not care a whit about what another coalition member thought about white supremacy, only what the person was willing to do to advance the criminal justice cause. I realized right then that much of the progressive coalition work had become more committed to applying ideological litmus tests than to addressing real world problems.

Controlling the Discourse

Jewish volunteer leaders were often not as quick as their professional counterparts to parse the new racial justice discourse; some were privately critical of the new ideology, and some were confused about all the new terms and concepts they were hearing for the first time. "What does 'decolonize' mean?" one volunteer asked me. Another wondered, "What do they mean by 'white supremacy'.... Is this different from the KKK?" So I decided to write a "Glossary of Social Justice Terms: A Guide for the Perplexed," which we could share with our network of agencies. I looked for examples of such glossaries and discovered that they invariably used woke terms to define woke terms. The Multicultural Resource Center of Amherst College's "Race and Ethnicity Terms & Definitions,"[57] for example, defined "Anti-Blackness" as "behaviors, attitudes and practices of people and institutions that work to dehumanize Black people in order to maintain white supremacy." I wanted our glossary to define these terms as simply and clearly as possible. I shared my draft of the glossary with several staff members and asked for their input. They were uncharacteristically slow to reply. Finally, two weeks later, Melanie, the senior vice president, told me I should get feedback from Tammy, a Progressive young staff person who was active in various Progressive coalitions and attuned to the discourse. Tammy sent me back a draft of the Glossary that reinstated all the self-referential language I was trying to sweep out. "I see what you are trying to do here, David," she stated diplomatically. "But I think it's a huge mistake to strip down these definitions, which would cause us problems with our partners in the civil rights community." I could have overruled her but would have faced fierce opposition from the rest of the staff. The Glossary never saw the light of day.

Tammy may have been right about the likely reaction from coalition members. Why, however, would anyone get up in arms over making our terms clear? In the Fall of 2020, a leading figure among Jews of color told my colleagues and me that we should stop using the term "Black-Jewish relations" because the term suggests a false binary, that being Jewish means not being Black. "What should we call this work then," I asked? "That's for you to figure out," she said, a common refrain from woke ideologues putting the onus back on the non-marginalized person. "If we can't use the term Black-Jewish relations," I complained to my colleagues, "how can we do the work of Black-Jewish relations?" No one seemed to have an answer. Marc Dollinger, in his book *Black Power Jewish Politics*, writes that "Jews of color challenged the Black-Jewish dichotomy at its most basic level. What if what is Black is also Jewish? What if Jews are in fact Black?"[58] I found the entire line of reasoning absurd. The fact that there are Indian Americans, for example, does not mean that merely speaking about US-India relations "erases" Indian Americans in the US. The fact that certain people's identities straddle boundaries doesn't mean that the boundaries don't exist or aren't useful. The false dichotomy is not "Black-Jewish," it's the idea that Black-Jewish relations and Black Jews are mutually exclusive concepts. This concern about Black Jews struck me not so much as a legitimate gripe by a marginalized person as it did a power grab by someone trying to buck the supposed white-Jewish establishment.

Was the woke preoccupation with language, I wondered, a genuine expression of support for marginalized people, or a cynical word game meant to delegitimize the system of "white supremacy"? After all, woke ideology is the practical application of postmodernism, a mode of thought that blurs boundaries as a means of tearing down power structures. Maybe woke ideologues deal in such word games not to prevent the erasure of Black Jews, but instead to disrupt a perceived white power structure. If Jewish communal leaders can't use the term Black-Jewish relations, then we can't do Black-Jewish relations; if we can't do Black-Jewish relations, then we can't perform the organization's mission. Maybe the words weren't the problem, but I and others like me—males in charge—were the problem, and disrupting us was the point. If everything we said in addressing social issues was constantly "problematized"—that is, if we were constantly subjected to the specious postmodern practice of finding and exaggerating problems in discourses—then eventually we would fall into a state of linguistic chaos and paralysis: a contemporary version of the Tower of Babel, where people yell their heads off but cannot hear others or make themselves heard. So, like the Tower, the current leadership would collapse. And maybe, I thought, that was precisely what they had in mind in relentlessly challenging the language. Whatever the case, I was growing weary of all the chaos, the demands for deference, the micro-cancellations. Increasingly I yearned—like the signatories of the *Harper's* letter—to stand up for open and free discourse and to fight this ideological scourge, not to pretend that I supported it.

CHAPTER 7

GOODBYE, DOUBLETHINK!

Doublethinker?

One of my heroes is Natan Sharansky, the former Soviet Refusenik of the 1970s and 1980s, who spent nine years in the Gulag for his human rights activism. Upon his release from the Soviet Union, he became an Israeli politician and a best-selling author. Sharansky speaks about a phenomenon, first described by George Orwell in *1984*, that Sharansky knew well in the Soviet Union: "doublethink," which occurs when people pretend to believe in something they don't. "Double thinkers did not become dissidents because it was too dangerous," Sharansky said. "They could have been killed. So they kept their critical opinions of the regime to themselves and lived in a constant state of self-censorship." Unlike in the Soviet Union, however, in today's America you cannot blame a dictator for preventing you from speaking. "No one is forcing you into doublethink. No one will disappear you. Freedom of expression depends only on the courage of your convictions," he stated.[59] Had I become a doublethinker? In the wake of George Floyd's death, reluctant to voice my views, I began to wonder.

The McWhorter Test

In the summer and fall of 2020, Batya Ungar-Sargon, a self-described leftist and opinion editor at the national Jewish publication, *The Forward*, wrote a series of articles on diverse Black thinkers who opposed woke ideology. Though she had once subscribed to them herself, Ungar-Sargon had grown skeptical of woke claims and disturbed by the increasingly censorious environment in the Jewish community. She wrote about "a small group of Black intellectuals (such as John McWhorter, Thomas Chatterton Williams, Kmele Foster, Chloe Valdary, Glenn Loury, and Coleman Hughes) who are leading a counter-culture against the newly hegemonic wokeness."[60] While each of these politically diverse thinkers fully acknowledges the scourge of racism, none buys into the current woke, "anti-racist" contention that America is pervasively racist today.

In June 2021, Ungar-Sargon told me in a podcast interview that she wrote *The Forward* articles out of the sense that Jews are in a state of moral confusion. "The Jewish community right now is in a crisis of moral authority around race," she told me. "They have lost the idea of what it means to be a Jew. And the reason is in anti-racism work—the critical race theory model—there's no objective sense of morality. They replaced morality with power. Powerlessness has become the moral position of our time, which is evidenced by belonging to a marginalized group. And what this means is that a person who has more power, who is less marginalized, no longer has the right to a moral position in society. That right has to be ceded to a person with less power. That means that Jews, 92 percent of whom, according to the latest Pew study, identify as white, feel that they no longer have the right to their own moral position. I totally reject that. Our job as Jews is to distinguish right from wrong."[61] I read the same Black authors, listened to the same podcasts and came to the same conclusion as Ungar-Sargon: The Jewish community was getting a very one-sided view of the Black community and contorting its values to conform. It badly needed to hear alternative Black voices.

For the "crime" of highlighting non-woke points of view in her writing, Ungar-Sargon endured a torrent of protests, some demanding her head, even though she was an opinion editor supposedly with broad leeway to express her own views. I too wanted to introduce the Jewish community to some of the same Black thinkers but concluded that I couldn't pull it off. Had I attempted to do so, I would have faced stiff resistance, first from my own staff, then from a handful of Board members with outsized influence, then from a few shrill local directors, and finally from progressive leaders of member organizations who might well have accused me of platforming racists. Now, when I think of what success would look like in restoring sanity to Jewish institutions and others, I invoke the "McWhorter Test": would an organization be able to invite Black heterodox thinker and *New York Times* columnist John McWhorter to speak on issues of race and not get canceled? If and when the answer is yes, we will have made progress.

Here I was, the head of a national Jewish umbrella organization, and I couldn't even feature a Black speaker who didn't go along with the Progressive consensus on race. So instead, we platformed only speakers on race who toed the party line. No wonder many people mistakenly believe that nearly all Blacks hold the same views on matters of race and racism. In my inability to open up the conversation on race, I had become Sharansky's "doublethinker." Ungar-Sargon left *The Forward* in December 2020 to become the deputy opinion editor of *Newsweek*, which lately has served as a platform for heterodox thinkers challenging woke ideology. She also came out with a highly touted book, *Bad News: How Woke Media Is Undermining Democracy*.

What's in a Name?

In the summer of 2020, the progressive Jewish group Bend the Arc circulated an open letter of unqualified support for Black Lives Matter. The JCPA was asked to sign on. The letter read:

> "Black Lives Matter the recent uprisings across the globe in the wake of the murders of Breonna Taylor, Ahmaud Arbery, George Floyd, Rayshard Brooks, and so many others, and the decades of political organizing across the country that have led to this moment are movements led by and for Black people."[62]

The poorly worded screed equated the phrase "Black Lives Matter" with the protests, not the official organization that bore its name and not the literal meaning of those three words: that the lives of Black people matter. Did I really support the 2020 BLM protests: calls to "Defund the Police"; white people taking a knee, prostrating themselves before Black protestors to atone for their supposed complicity in white supremacy;

demands that casual diners make the Black Lives Matter fist sign; or the violent attacks on police buildings?

No, I did not support any of that behavior. I did and do sympathize, however, with peaceful protests, the pain so many Black people feel as a result of the legacy of racism in America, and the continued racial disparities in so many walks of life. I had no idea, however, what Black Lives Matter was asking me to support—a phrase? An organization? A policy platform? Specific protests? One evening in 2020, while walking in Midtown Manhattan, I happened upon a BLM march of about 200 people. The marchers yelled loudly and repeatedly, as one voice, "Fuck the Police!" "This is the civil rights movement of our time?" I thought to myself. Missing from the angry chants was a vision for a better, more humane society—the very hallmark of the civil rights movement of the 1960s.

Marc Dollinger, a professor of Jewish Studies at San Francisco State University and the author of *Black Power, Jewish Politics*, stated that "there is widespread support for the Black Lives Matter movement among white Jews.... This is something we didn't even see in the '60s. This is more impressive."[63] I didn't see the current level of Jewish support as impressive at all: so much Jewish backing struck me as pure performance, mass virtue-signaling powerfully enforced by a Progressive minority, so that the only possible course of action for any individual or group was unconditional endorsement.

That's what happens when, as Ungar-Sargon said, the Jewish community is morally adrift and defers to others for moral authority. As time went on it became clear that if Black Lives Matter stood for anything, it was "Defund the Police," which Jewish and moderate civil rights leaders chose to interpret figuratively as a call to downsize the role of the police in society, but which BLM activists meant literally, as did the cities that subsequently slashed police budgets. The prospect of signing Bend the Arc's open letter of unqualified support for BLM made my head spin; although I personally opposed the starry-eyed proclamation, I could not think of a single reason JCPA shouldn't sign the letter, given the stance the organization had taken since George Floyd's death. I had led the organization on cruise control, unable—or unwilling, I couldn't tell which—to deviate from the Progressive party line. Resigned to my plight, I endorsed the letter in a small task force meeting of JCPA Board members, and the organization indicated its support that evening. In late August of 2020, the letter was published as an ad in the *New York Times* with over 600 Jewish denominations, organizations, and synagogues. And I felt like a doublethinker.

Honestly

In October of 2020, Bari Weiss published a widely circulated and hard-hitting piece in *Tablet Magazine* called "Stop Being Shocked." A few months earlier, Weiss had left her post as op-ed staff editor and writer on culture and politics at the *New York Times* in a fury with a scathing open letter to the newspaper's publisher in which she said she had been bullied by colleagues in an "illiberal environment," noting that she didn't understand how such toxic behavior was allowed in the newsroom.[64] In her *Tablet* article, Weiss described the increasingly illiberal atmosphere in Progressive circles and mainstream institutions. "It makes sense that many smart, well-intentioned people are confused," she stated.[65] "Or rather: Looking for someone to explain why an emerging movement that purports to advance the ideals they have always supported—fairness, justice, righting historical wrongs—feels like it is doing the opposite." But then she turned her wrath on Jewish organizations—like mine—that had been actively engaging woke Progressives. "Funders and communal leaders who are falling over themselves to make alliances with fashionable activists and ideas enjoy a decadent indulgence," she stated. "That leaders and philanthropists charged to protect and nurture our community are entertaining, and at times embracing, such nihilistic and anti-American ideas is a scandal."

Several colleagues of mine in the Jewish advocacy world shared with me their dismay at the positive reception that Weiss's article received in some Jewish quarters. While I agreed wholeheartedly with her searing critique of woke ideology, I still clung to the notion that Jewish organizations had an interest in engaging Progressive forces, if for no other reason than to influence their thinking about Jews and Israel. I engaged Weiss in a discussion over email, hoping that she would agree to publish a version of the exchange. I told her privately that I was "IDW through and through." (IDW stands for "Intellectual Dark Web," a term that was briefly in fashion to describe people, mostly liberals, who opposed woke ideology. Months earlier, Weiss had written a controversial article about the nascent movement in the *Times*.[66]) I also made the case for Jewish leaders who shared her critique of the illiberal environment (i.e., me) but still felt it was important to show up in Progressive spaces and defend Jewish interests. She didn't buy it and didn't agree to go public with our email exchanges. Once again, I had the strange sensation that I was acting as a Jewish organizational avatar, no longer accurately representing my authentic self. Did *I* really believe it was in the Jewish community's interest to place so much emphasis on engaging progressive ideologues? No, *I* did not. Did *I* think mainstream Jewish groups were increasingly paying a price for surfing the current Progressive ideological wave? Yes, *I* did.

An Un-stealthy Pseudonym

By that time, I was ablaze with determination to oppose the ascending woke ideology and to relieve myself of the excruciating predicament of doublethink. So in November of 2020, I published the first of numerous articles while still in my professional role at JCPA: "The Dangers of Woke Harm-based Morality," in *Areo*, a liberal humanist publication, under the least stealthy pseudonym in human history: "David Bern."[67] (I could not find another David Bern on Google; "Bern" was not really a name, not even a truncated, anglicized Jewish name like Gold or Rosen, but it was the only thing I could think of.) I also started an anonymous Twitter account, UnwokeBlog, that Twitter somehow translated as @BlogUnwoke. Awkward, but I didn't care. I felt alive and energized, finally able to express my true beliefs, even if under the pretense of a false name. My wife, in a state of disbelief, asked: "Seriously? 'David Bern'—that's the best you could come up with?" I couldn't really answer her question. Maybe I subconsciously wanted to get caught and end all the doublethink. Despite my recklessness, I never did get busted for writing those articles in my final months at JCPA.

An Equity Cartoon

Late that December, tensions were running high between me and several Board members who firmly supported the anti-racist ideology, and wanted the organization's policy to reflect it. In a call with these Board members about a policy statement the organization was mulling over on racial justice, I raised concerns about the term "equity," which was cited repeatedly in the draft racial justice document. "The concept of equity is not just another word for equality," I stated. "Ibram X. Kendi defines equity as when all groups are approximately on equal footing in any institution or endeavor."

"Is there a problem with that?" a Board member asked me.

"There's a reason that there are more male coal miners than women coal miners, and it's not discrimination," I stated. "Likewise, not all groups have the same levels of average educational achievement so it's unrealistic to think that there will be, say, 13 percent Black scientists when there aren't anywhere near 13 percent Black science students. What we really need is to invest in STEM for minorities so in the long run there are more Black scientists." Silence.

Then, "I really like that 'Equality versus Equity' cartoon," another Board member interjected, with a smile. "The one with three people trying to watch a baseball game over a fence, standing on wooden boxes. In the cartoon, Equality gives everyone the same sized wooden box to stand on to watch the game over the fence, but it's not high enough for the shortest of the three people, who still can't see the game. In Equity, the shortest person received an additional wooden box to stand on so all three people were high up enough to watch the game." I had seen that puerile representation of equity circulating on social media. A spoof of the cartoon showed, under Equity, all three of the people standing at the fence, two with their legs chopped off so that they were the same size as the shortest person; none of them could see over the fence.

I fully agreed with the message of the spoof: an equity regime would produce a drive to the bottom that wouldn't serve anyone, especially the people on the lowest socio-economic rung. Interestingly, according to Rabbi Yitz Greenberg, one of today's greatest living Jewish theologians, the Kendi version of equity is at odds with the Jewish tradition. He wrote in *Sapir*—a Jewish journal of ideas—in Spring 2021:

> On one hand, the Torah repeatedly warns about injustice to the poor: "You shall not pervert judgment of the poor in his cause" (Exodus 23:6)…On the other hand, one must not pursue justice through unjust means: "You shall not favor a poor man in his cause [unjustly]" (Exodus 23:3); and "you shall not do unrighteousness in judgment [or policy]" (Leviticus 19:15). The Torah is warning against twisting our basic moral code on behalf of the oppressed. We cannot compromise our principles to assert that the oppressed are just regardless of their behavior, simply because of their identity. Their race, gender, past colonial status, membership in a marginalized group, and so forth, do not a priori make their cause right and all opposition to it wrong. Where a free society ought to engage in policy debates, we instead find ourselves in the midst of quasi-religious battles between good and evil.

Already in a politically fraught predicament, I did not share my impression of the Equity cartoon with the Board members. Instead, I argued that the equity concept runs counter to the traditional American equality narrative, and that it would make everyone worse off. I warned that equity might be weaponized against Jews and Asians, in particular, whose success makes them appear "white-adjacent." "If someone is kept down because of white supremacy, someone else must have been propped up by it," I said. "Jews will be seen as profiting at the expense of Black people."

"I don't see it that way," stated another Board member in a tone of finality that made it obvious the conversation was over. I suspect that the Board members did not want to spend much time openly debating the concept of equity in this intimate setting, let alone in a larger setting, where the organization would be vulnerable to criticism merely for holding the discussion.

This controversy-avoidant dynamic on racial issues short-circuited our customary deliberative process. Jewish organizations like the JCPA could spend hours debating the most minute detail—a single word—in a policy statement, with motions and counter-motions into the wee hours of the night. But racial issues—as important as they were—were too hot to handle, even if no one dared say so. While nobody on the call was uncivil, it became very clear to me that I was not on the same page as these Board members. I reckoned that my willingness to question the racial pieties made me at best out of sync, and at worse a perceived heretic, endangering JCPA's credibility.

Don't Talk about Portland

In October 2020, amid a global pandemic, President Trump made it clear that he might not accept the national election results. Rabbi Doug Kahn—formerly the highly respected director of the Jewish Community Relations Council of San Francisco and now a consultant—warned early that Trump might oppose Biden's election, and that the country would enter a period of political turmoil and violence. Under such conditions, he said, JCPA would need to provide high-level expert advice to its network on what to say and do. I agreed, and we assembled a task force of respected election lawyers, security experts, political hands, and PR professionals to guide us through this tumultuous period. As predicted, the President did challenge the validity of the election. On a December Zoom call after the election, while discussing the potential for violence, I stated that while the current focus is properly on the elections, we should also pay attention to the violence on the left as well. "We really do have to take seriously the attacks on police precincts and the creation of these autonomous zones in Portland and Seattle...." I was immediately shouted down. "Those aren't the same thing!" bellowed one of the participants. Others nodded in disgust at the mere mention of left-wing violence. They were willing to give barbarity a pass on the extremes of their own political tribe. I no longer felt I belonged in such "Progressive" circles.

Books, Not Bibles

Toward the end of December, I spoke at several Jewish Federation Board meetings on Zoom. The Federation heads were getting pushback from key stakeholders who were increasingly ill at ease with unqualified support for BLM, which still had a platform on its website that accused Israel of genocide. Nor did the spectacle of BLM and Antifa activists taking over several city blocks and carving out autonomous zones sit well with many liberal Jewish suburbanites.

My job was to provide a moderate case for continued mainstream Jewish engagement with progressive movements and Black Lives Matter. In one Federation Board meeting over Zoom, a woman tentatively asked me about two books the community relations committee of the Federation was asked to read by the staff: Robin DiAngelo's *White Fragility* and Ibram X. Kendi's *How to Be an Anti-Racist.* Book clubs across the country were reading and discussing these texts as part of the great racial reckoning. I privately thought that the books were intellectually stultifying. I didn't see how anyone could take seriously Robin DiAngelo's concept of "White Women's Tears," her critique of "white people's laments."[68] Her thesis that any challenge to her pronouncements on race somehow constituted "fragility" struck me as both ludicrous and—well, fragile.

"What do you think of those books?" the Board member asked. I took a breath. "I think they are books, not Bibles. And if we are treating them as Bibles, then we are promoting a kind of religion. And I already have a religion that I don't always believe in." After a brief pause came a torrent of applause. A man emboldened by my last reply then asked me skeptically: "What do you think of this idea of systemic racism?" I answered: "I think there are still places in American life with deeply embedded racism. However," I paused, then stated slowly, "there is a difference between saying there is systemic racism in America, and saying that America is systemically racist." Then more applause this time. I was buoyed by the response. "All they needed was a little leadership," I thought to myself.

In February of 2021, I announced that I was leaving JCPA and dedicating myself to advancing classical liberal values. I posted on Facebook:

> While I continue to believe deeply in social justice, I am very concerned about the rise of "critical social justice," out of which grows cancel culture. I am, at core, a liberal humanist who strongly supports the free exchange of ideas as the foundation of a liberal society. A free society encourages rational argument and prompts people of different views to engage in authentic discussion. Such a culture of debate and rational discourse is how we solve problems and grow knowledge. It's how we elevate good ideas and root out bad ones.
>
> Some of what I write and say publicly from here on out may seem controversial. It shouldn't. I should be able to oppose systemic racism in America without conceding that America is systemically racist. I should be able to say without fear of reprisal that despite all its faults America is the most successful experiment in pluralism in human history. And make no mistake, people cannot say those things in many settings without risking their livelihoods or reputations or ostracism. Cancel culture sounds like it would be a raucous affair. But its primary sound is silence. That won't change until more of us who believe in free discourse speak out.

I knew my next step professionally would involve supporting free expression and open discourse, although I had no firm job offers. I did, however, have peace of mind, knowing I would no longer be squirming in doublethink. And in the future, I would help other disillusioned doublethinkers find the courage of their convictions.

CHAPTER 8

CANCEL CULTURE, JEWISH STYLE

Coming Out

After I left JCPA in February 2021, determined to express my concerns over mounting illiberalism in the Jewish community, I interviewed with two mainstream Jewish media outlets, the Jewish Telegraphic Agency (JTA) and *eJewish Philanthropy*, but both interviews mysteriously failed to materialize. (Subsequently, however, *eJewish Philanthropy* did publish several opinion pieces I wrote.). I then took my story to the conservative Jewish News Service (JNS), whose editor, Jonathan Tobin, interviewed me and published "Can liberalism be saved from cancel culture?"[69] in March 2021.

"According to Bernstein," Tobin wrote, "the last year, since the death of George Floyd set off a summer of Black Lives Matter demonstrations, an already growing willingness among liberal Jews and their institutions to embrace critical race theory has gotten out of control." The Jewish left reacted quickly. Jill Jacobs, CEO of T'ruah, the Rabbinic Call for Human Rights, tweeted: "David, the fact that the primary far right-wing media voice in the Jewish world is congratulating you should give you pause. Tobin is not interested in ending racism, in justice or equity—he's interested in smearing the left, and I'm afraid that you're helping him." I later learned that because the mainstream press refuses to cover them, liberals and moderates who are critical of Progressive ideology often end up on conservative media outlets, only to be slammed by Progressives for getting coverage where they can. Author Kara Dansky, whose work expresses concerns about gender ideology from a feminist perspective, observed, "I would love to have a conversation with *The New York Times*, with *The Washington Post*, with MSNBC, CNN. I would love to do that. They are not, seemingly, willing to even have a conversation about this, so I go on conservative media because conservative media will have me." [70]

Following Jacobs' tweet, there was an outpouring of criticism and disparagement, mainly from Progressive rabbis who are part of her network. I knew that many rabbis from the liberal denominations loosely subscribed to woke diktats, but I didn't realize how steeped in the ideology they were. I worried about what would happen if they continued to proselytize the Jewish community unopposed. In one exchange, Yehudah Kurtzer, President of the Hartman Institute of North America, accused me of speaking from a place of privilege because I critiqued cancel culture. The fact that I had previously headed a national Jewish organization apparently disqualified me in his eyes from commenting on the stifling and censorious ideological environment. Kurtzer then suggested, if you can create an organization supported by the community, go ahead. "Hmmmm," I thought, "maybe that's what I ought to do." Until that point it hadn't occurred to me to start an organization devoted to countering illiberalism in the Jewish community.

Someone Else's Turn

In the response to the JNS article, I was especially surprised at how rabbis and other progressive Jewish leaders had embraced the notion that it's someone else's exclusive turn to speak. Rabbi Jonah Geffen, Senior Jewish Educator and Campus Rabbi at Hunter College Hillel, tweeted, "To achieve equity of voice, some voices will be amplified and to make space in the discourse others, who in the past took up more space, necessarily take up less. This is not 'canceling'.... What's hard about equity is that to get there some will have to step back, not dictate, not orchestrate. And that will feel like loss, but it's not." Another prominent Progressive Jew, Isaac Luria, Director of Voice, Creativity and Culture at the Nathan Cummings Foundations, added: "Like I trust a plumber to fix a broken pipe, I trust Black people to describe the impact of American racism.

The idea that this is somehow illiberal feels bizarre and defensive. We're welcome to our opinions as white men but you're [i.e., me] not welcome to unchallenged expertise." Luria's comment was a classical expression of standpoint epistemology—the idea that knowledge is derived from one's position in the power hierarchy. I agree with Kurzer, Geffen, and Luria that society has a special obligation to listen to the experiences of marginalized people. I strongly disagree, however, that obligates anyone to defer to anyone else or to just keep quiet.

Their comments were precisely what Batya Ungar-Sargon warned against: a crisis in moral authority whereby Jews cede their moral voice to others. Geffen insists that this deference is not "canceling," but it is precisely that: in his conception, someone must dictate who has standing to speak and who doesn't, which ideas get voiced and heard, and which ideas get downplayed or even rejected. Such an assumption of authority is inherently illiberal and restricts speech. Invalidating someone's opinion based on their perceived place in the intersectional hierarchy—their "positionality"—is, in fact, the ideological foundation of cancel culture. Mainstream Jews, as well, have not been immune from making standpoint claims in defining antisemitism for society. Popular Jewish writer Sarah Tuttle-Singer, for example, tweeted, "Here is a complete and comprehensive list of the people who get to decide what is or isn't anti-Semitic: 1. Jews." They're wrong to do so as well.

To be fair, not all woke ideologues explicitly deny the right of non-marginalized voices to partake in the discussion. I doubt the likes of Geffen and Luria would go that far. But the *effect* of these claims on who has standing to speak is to police the conversation and to silence dissenting voices. Exhortations that formerly powerful people, especially white males, step back sets a culture of discourse that is inimical to freedom of speech. People who demand that others—John McWhorter calls them "The Elect"—"make space"[71] may not shut down the conversation altogether, but the conversation surely will shut down, if for no other reason than that shriller voices will do the moderates' bidding, acting on the moral imperative that it's someone else's turn to talk. Woke ideology is a radical's pathway to power. As we've seen repeatedly over the decades, woke ideology picks up steam when moderate ideologues pave the way for more extreme ideologues, and moderate illiberalism gives rise to more extreme illiberalism.

Not only are such standpoint claims illiberal, they're also divorced from reality. First, not all "marginalized" voices agree with each other. For example, Black people—like all people—are politically diverse. According to Pew Research, more than 60 percent of Black people oppose affirmative action in higher education.[72] The vast majority aren't woke. The woke notion of "making space" tends to mean platforming minority voices that reflect progressive pieties and ignoring or pillorying all the rest. Second, marginalized people—like all people—are sometimes wrong. Some impart earth-shattering truths while others spread lies and become bullies and predators themselves. Lived experience, while important, is just one data point in understanding social reality. As a Jewish person who has experienced antisemitism, I have insight into Jew-hatred that others should listen to. But I cannot have the final say. There are other data points as well: a Pew Survey, for example, showed that Jews are the most admired religious community in America. That, too, is a data point worth considering. Third, insisting that large swaths of people take a back seat to others is not a sustainable moral or political undertaking. The polling on woke ideology is clear: large majorities of all age groups, races, genders, and religions abhor it.[73] By making itself so unpopular, Progressive ideology actually makes government less progressive. Calling on those deemed privileged to mute themselves on issues of race and racism engenders resentment, which in turn gets expressed on Election Day in the privacy of the ballot box. Finally, once you adopt someone else's prepackaged reality, you've outsourced your values to a third party who may make absurd statements or engage in untenable behavior down the line that you will feel compelled to defend. Numerous Jewish organizations have done just that, a subject I will return to later.

Founding JILV

In my first opinion piece for *eJewish Philanthropy* after leaving JCPA, "Six questions Jewish organizations should contemplate before taking a stand on racial and critical social justice," I wrote:

> I have long championed Jewish engagement in racial justice movements.... I support criminal justice and police reform and believe that there is racism—some of it systemic—in American society. Nevertheless, I believe that the Critical Social Justice (CSJ) ideology (i.e., woke ideology) that frequently comes packaged with these movements can have a corrupting influence on Jewish organizational values. It often insists on its own absolute inviolability, a hallmark of an illiberal dogma; shuts down discourse; and indoctrinates.

I then listed six questions Jewish organizations should ask themselves, such as "Do you believe America is a white supremacist society? How does that perspective comport with the previously common understanding of America as a pluralistic democracy that has sometimes failed to live up to its ideals?"[74] This article, too, struck a nerve. One former colleague called me on the phone to tell me a progressive colleague of ours had read the article and called me "David Bull Connor Bernstein."

Perhaps, as some suggested, I needed to sugarcoat my call for open discussion on racial issues so Progressives could hear me. Or, as others suggested, Progressives perceived my ideas as threatening precisely because I presented them so fastidiously. I'm still not sure of the answer. Whatever the case, the opposition from the Progressive Jewish camp to that first article clinched it: I would start a new project to support liberal values in the Jewish community. The Jewish Institute for Liberal Values (JILV) came into being when I discussed my idea with a leading Jewish philanthropist, who instantly provided a $25,000 gift to get the initiative off the ground. "By the way," he said, "I know you got a lot of flak for the article in *eJewish Philanthropy*. I liked it."

In May 2021, I launched "A Letter to Our Fellow Jews on Equality and Liberal Values,"[75] also known as the Jewish *Harper's* Letter, signed originally by fifty prominent Jews and later by more than 1000 others. Rabbi David Wolpe, Bari Weiss, Bret Stephens, Pamela Paresky, Monica Osborne, and I co-authored the Letter. My friend Dan—the same college friend I had yelled at for wearing the "Men Rape, Men Can Stop Rape" button—built the JILV website and helped assemble the infrastructure of the new organization. The Letter became the defining manifesto of the new organization, reading in part:

> The American Jewish community is facing a challenge to the liberal principles that have long defined Jewish civic life and America's democratic tradition. Today this freedom is being threatened. An ideology is taking hold across the country that insists there is only one way to look at the problems we face, and those who disagree must be silenced. This suppression of dissent violates the core Jewish value of open discourse. Jewish tradition cherishes debate, respects disagreement, and values questions as well as answers.

The Letter received extensive press coverage, as well as its fair share of support and opposition on social media. *The Forward*'s Arno Rosenfeld called me to ask how the new initiative was funded. I had read Rosenfeld's conspiracy-laden articles in the past, and after consulting with others in the Jewish community familiar with his work, decided not to speak with him. True to form, his article, "Jewish '*Harper's* Letter Tied to Opaque Foundation, Republican megadonor," claimed that "dark money" and "questionable partners" lay behind the JILV: "The Jewish Institute for Liberal Values is a project of an opaque foundation connected to Republican megadonor Adam Beren," Rosenfeld alleged.[76] No dark money in JILV, but plenty of yellow journalism by Rosenfeld. Adam Beren, the donor behind the Combat Hate Foundation, generously agreed to have his foundation serve as a fiscal sponsor for the JILV until we were officially approved by the IRS so that we could receive and disburse funds. We received no funding from him or his foundation. At the time of *The Forward* article, JILV had received financial commitments of a grand total of $50,000, not a penny of which had been spent. What's more, there was nothing "opaque" about the Combat Hate Foundation, which had yet to list its assets because it wasn't registered as a nonprofit until 2020, and had not yet filed the requisite tax forms. Such would be the case with any foundation, no matter where it stood politically. One thing was clear here, though: the mainstream Jewish press, with few exceptions, was not going to give us a fair shake.

Private Messages

After we launched the JILV, I immediately began to receive private messages from Jewish professionals, who shared their anguish and exasperation in the stifling cultures of their workplaces or in the broader Progressive Jewish arena. One professional in a mainstream organization was forced by his organization's management to undergo diversity training for making comments that were clearly misunderstood. He showed me the email that had landed him in trouble. I was aghast that anyone would consider his innocuous remarks offensive. (I'm not sharing the content so as to protect his anonymity). Fed up, he found a new job in another organization. He had originally agreed to come on the JILV podcast to discuss the incident and his larger concerns about the ideological environment, but he ducked out at the last minute: "Someone (from my current organization) was just fired for saying the wrong thing," he wrote. "I can't chance it."

On another occasion, a rabbi contacted me privately to get my take on "cancel culture" after he read some of the JILV material I had sent out. He stated in an email, "To be honest, some of what I see here doesn't resonate with me, but I respect you a lot and am sure I could learn from hearing your thinking." We then scheduled a time and spoke about Critical Race Theory, which he had studied for many years and uses in his teaching. "I do agree it is often being used in a rigid manner," he said. I told him that I thought CRT was a completely valid theoretical lens that has given me insights about the world I would not otherwise have. But, I explained, "I think it's not being used just in a rigid way but in a stifling way." Most of its adherents are insisting CRT is the only valid way of understanding social and economic disparities, which prevents genuine dialogue that considers alternative views.

The rabbi and I were in more agreement than either of us had assumed about the nature of the current discourse. I had a more nuanced view on CRT than he had imagined, and he had a more complex one than I had imagined. I asked the rabbi if he would join me on the JILV podcast to model the thoughtful and respectful dialogue we had just had. "People need to hear this nuanced conversation," I told him.

He paused. "I'd have to think about it because I might hurt some people," he told me. I assured him that I understood. I later realized that his reluctance to speak to me in public was precisely the barrier we face in today's discourse; he inadvertently validated my critique of cancel culture. I am not accusing the rabbi of canceling me. I completely understand his reluctance; he could have been subjected to real-world consequences just for speaking with me. But he decided not to speak to me in the open because if he did, he would put certain key professional and personal relationships at risk. Those who would claim to be hurt could possibly have penalized him for talking with me—not, mind you, for agreeing with me, but just for speaking with me—are shutting down open discussion of pressing cultural issues. In this case, they successfully prevented a rabbi, whose life work is to model the values of civil and ethical discourse, from doing that work.

Jewish Miseducation

One of JILV's first orders of business was to take a close look at Jewish day schools. Numerous day school parents told us of their concerns: that their kids were being indoctrinated in woke anti-racist ideology and taught that they were complicit in white supremacy. Brandy Shufutinsky, a Black Jewish woman then on the JILV Board and now JILV's Director of Education and Community Outreach, came across ideologically charged material and resources on the website of Charles E. Smith Jewish Day School in Rockville, Maryland, one of the flagship pluralistic day schools in the US. Both Brandy and I had once had children in the school. Like so many others, the school's diversity program did not provide alternative perspectives to the woke "anti-racist" point of view. Brandy and I regarded this pedagogy as indoctrination. We co-wrote an Open Letter raising concerns about the school's "Diversity, Equity, Inclusion and Justice" (DEIJ) program, expressing our concern about "the lack of critical thinking and intellectual openness evident in the CESJDS DEIJ Framework."[77]

I decided to post this Open Letter on JEDLAB, a Jewish educators' Facebook group with 12,000 members. In 2012, I was active in the early days of JEDLAB, a space where innovative educators shared and discussed cutting-edge ideas and approaches, often at odds with the Jewish educational establishment. I loved JEDLAB so much I even interviewed the founder in an article for *eJewish Philanthropy*. JEDLAB seemed a perfect forum for generating interesting and important discussion about emerging diversity programs in Jewish educational settings. Apparently, however, DEI initiatives in Jewish schools are not open for discussion. Almost immediately, a member of the Facebook group pronounced my post "racist" and said I had no business posting my views on the JEDLAB page. Several others piled on, repeating the charge of racism and urging its immediate removal. Not a single Jewish educator took exception or came to my defense—except in private messages.

About an hour after I put it up, and scores of comments later, the page's administrators removed it without explanation. I conjured two possible explanations: First, the administrators all felt that anyone who raised concerns about the woke "anti-racist" perspective taught to kids must be inherently racist; Ibram X. Kendi had spoken, and we must all fall in line—in which case, I despaired over the future of Jewish education. Second, the administrators had received complaints that my criticisms of DEI made the space "unsafe" for participants. This, of course, meant that the administrators had to silence anyone with a different point of view so that others could feel safe. This is the "heckler's veto": a few shrill voices who protest a particular viewpoint can make spineless institutions fall in line and stifle discourse. If that was the case, I again despaired over the future of Jewish education.

Our kids should be educated in a cultural sensibility that values *Makhloket Leshem Shamayim*: "arguments for the sake of heaven." This sensibility welcomes—even encourages—debate among thinkers with different points of view. The Jewish penchant to question and engage in intellectual discourse is a central attribute of Jewish tradition. Why would anyone, least of all Jewish educators, try to blot it out? Don't we want our kids to be critical thinkers and challenge the status quo? Of course, many Jewish educators and parents do value discussion among people with different viewpoints. A headmaster of a pluralistic Jewish school direct-messaged me on Facebook and thanked me for raising the topic. One prominent professor called me after he read the Open Letter to say, "I wanted to kiss you." Many Jewish day school teachers thanked me and my co-author for giving voice to their concerns. These teachers cannot speak publicly themselves because they fear they will be canceled, just like my Facebook post was.

In the *Jewish Journal*, I wrote about the experience in a piece called "Cancel Culture, Jewish Educators Style."[78] A few days later, not entirely unexpectedly, I received a note from Melissa Ser, an education director of a synagogue, who was on the "moderation team" of JEDLAB and wrote on the entire team's behalf. Amused by the hubris, I called my friend Michael and read him the message. "The Sanhendrin has spoken," I proclaimed. (The Sanhendrin were assemblies of seventy-one judges who sat on tribunals in ancient Israel.) I read : "After deliberations by the moderation team…we have made the decision to remove you from the Facebook group." The note then cited a litany of Jewish laws and ordinances I had supposedly broken, including "Do not profit by the blood of your friends" (Vayikra 19:16) and "Let the honor of our colleague be as dear to us as our own" (Avot D'Rabbi Natan 15:1). Nowhere on their list of Jewish values was *Makhloket Lashen Shamayim*, arguments for the sake of heaven—that cornerstone of the Jewish tradition. I told Ser that "a community that allows multiple members to attack me as racist without any defense and then removes the post, as if I am the problem, is not a community worth being part of." How many other Jews, I wondered, would be similarly alienated by a community that permitted such a narrow scope of opinion? And how would Jewish children fare being educated by teachers unwilling to countenance debate?

What's in a Letter

In order to build support for liberal values in the Jewish community, a small group of rabbis working with the JILV wrote a rabbis' letter, a "Committee of Concerned Rabbis," in the Fall of 2021. The letter stated, "Increasingly, the crowding out of unpopular opinions impinges upon society's ability to address problems.… Constricting conversation on social issues, including sensitive topics such as race and gender identity, makes it difficult, if not impossible, for society to formulate good policy, promote sound science, and resolve social tensions."[79] The letter was signed by 250 Reform and Conservative rabbis and included several prominent names. Unsurprisingly, the letter was panned by some of the same Progressive rabbis who had sought to discredit earlier such efforts. One Reform rabbi, Micah Streiffer tweeted: "At the risk of giving undue publicity to this thing.... I've read it [the rabbis' letter] four times and it just seems to be calling for space for bigoted & oppressive views to be aired. Maybe some of my colleagues who signed on can explain to me why??"

Rabbi Amy Wallk, a Conservative rabbi in Springfield, Massachusetts, and one of the original signatories, posted the letter on a listerv of Rabbinic colleagues. Wallk's twenty-two-year old son, Gabriel Katz, had recently been asked to leave the Moishe House, a collection of homes throughout the country for young Jewish adults. Gabriel's Moishe House roommates made it clear that they didn't want to live with a political conservative. Rather than siding with Gabriel, the staff of the Moishe House had reportedly backed the roommates, belying the organization's stated commitment to viewpoint diversity. Devastated, Gabriel moved out two weeks later.[80] Wallk was horrified by what had happened to her son, believing that Jewish institutions had a responsibility to uphold viewpoint diversity and liberal discourse. Several rabbis on the listerv expressed appreciation that Wallk shared her son's story and the Rabbis' Letter on the listserv; several lent their names to it. Another group, however, accused her of racism as well as transphobia—underscoring the purpose of the Letter in the first place—because the Letter stated that it's wrong to restrict conversations around sensitive topics like "gender identity." "They attacked my character and suggested somehow I was transphobic or homophobic or I really don't have sympathy for people of color," Wallk stated. "Nothing could be further from the truth." I knew how she felt: I was personally accused by one Reform rabbi of "targeting trans people."

***

Whether or not one calls these various occurrences—and I could cite many more—"cancel culture" is beside the point. They are evidence of a stifling, censorious and ideologically charged environment that flies in the face of the Jewish value of "arguments for the sake of heaven" and classical liberal values. They polarize our discourse and alienate many Jews from the Jewish enterprise. They make it more difficult to address problems in and out of the Jewish world and hamper the innovative spirit. "You can't have big and bold ideas if people can't say what they think,"[81] stated Felicia Herman, Maimonides Fund COO and managing editor of *Sapir*. "We all need space to be tentative, to be wrong and change our minds, to wonder, to explore," stated the signatories of the Rabbis' Letter. Today's muzzled discourse prevents such creativity. Even more concerning: these ideological predilections are being baked into Jewish organizational life.

CHAPTER 9

SLOUCHING TO WOKENESS

Identitarian Deference

Sometimes, we see the effects of woke ideology in brazen public acts, and sometimes in banal, everyday private interactions. In the Fall of 2021, I spoke with the CEO of a major Jewish foundation about the work of the Jewish Institute for Liberal Values. She asked me about JILV's success in recruiting moderates and political liberals into our work. "It's a challenge," I admitted, "because those on the center-left are often fearful of the consequences of being identified as opposing the ideology, and those on the center-right generally are not. We have to work much harder to bring in center-left people." I paused, then asked: "So where do you come down on all this?"

"I have come to believe that systemic racism is a very powerful force in society," she replied.

"I don't disagree," I said, "but shouldn't we be able to have open, thoughtful discussion and even disagreements about what racism explains and doesn't explain?"

"I really think systemic racism is a very important, defining quality of American life," she replied. "After George Floyd was murdered, the foundation team did a lot of soul searching. We hired a Jew of color to help us with diversity."

"Do you have any concerns about the current progressive discourse around race?" I asked.

She paused. "Well, sure, sometimes. But it's important that we empower Jews of color to help us navigate these challenges."

This was one of those seemingly low-key conversations that nevertheless spoke volumes about how deeply entrenched woke ideology had become in Jewish organizational life within just a matter of months. The foundation CEO did not say anything I hadn't heard before, but our conversation underscored for me how hard it will be to disentangle Jewish institutions and others from ideological and institutional commitments they made in the aftermath of George Floyd.

They signed on the proverbial dotted line of deference. In 2013, the writer Matt Bruenig coined the term "identitarian deference" (ID) to describe the concept that "privileged individuals should defer to the opinions and views of oppressed individuals, especially on topics relevant to those individuals' oppression." If standpoint epistemology theorizes that marginalized people have special insight into oppression, and thus the singular authority to define that oppression for the rest of society, then identitarian deference is the expression of standpoint doctrine in the behavior of institutions.

Jewish organizations—like other institutions—often defer to people with lived experience, mostly people of color with a Progressive political orientation, and young Jews whose delicate sensibilities—conventional wisdom has it—require constant, unequivocal validation, lest they leave the Jewish fold in droves. Bruenig argues that ID has become "so pervasive and so universally accepted in the liberal discourse that most commentators don't even seem capable of putting their finger on it. Instead, when ID generates abhorrent results, as it so often does, the liberal commentariat ends up grasping in the dark and then discussing a totally different topic."[82]

"The challenge with Identitarianism," Bruenig states, is "to figure out which oppressed voices to defer to." Bruenig points out that based on polls or surveys alone, it's often impossible to determine which Black/Latino/Asian American person to listen to: "Individuals in a particular oppressed group are not a monolith, and therefore necessarily disagree with one another." Pew Research Center polls show that even among Democrats, Blacks and Latinos are less likely to describe themselves as liberal than whites. An AP/NORC poll shows that the majority of Blacks are moderate (44 percent) or conservative (27 percent), and just 26 percent identify as liberal. As a result, Bruenig argues, most organizations just cherry-pick Black voices who will give the organization the political cover they are seeking. "What you can do," Bruenig observes, "is just figure out what you want to believe, and then find someone within the appropriate oppressed group who believes as you do. Then say that you are deferring to their voice in this matter." The foundation CEO and other Jewish leaders have done just that: they now characterize Black people as ideologically homogeneous, ignore any Black person who doesn't reflect the preferred consensus, and lift up that monolithic voice as both standard bearer and moral authority on all matters relating to race.

The impulse to defer to Progressive voices among people of color follows the pattern of another trend on the contemporary Jewish scene. The theory goes that if American Jewish life is to survive, the Jewish community needs to understand the "target audience"—young Jews—and design Jewish life around their social and political preferences. I don't altogether disagree with this mode of thinking: demographic and market research have their place in constructing experiences for younger Jews and other segments of the population. The Jewish community, however, has gone overboard in catering to the supposed Progressive sensibilities of young Jews, rather than to a broad range of preferences and viewpoints. Barry Shrage, the former charismatic CEO of the Combined Jewish Philanthropies (CJP) in Boston and Professor of Practice at Brandeis, told me, "A Jewish leader who checks a poll to see what everybody thinks, what the young people think before they decide on what they think and what they care about—that's such an abdication of leadership."[83]

It's also a fundamental inversion of Jewish tradition, from one that passes wisdom down from old to young, to one that passes wisdom up from young to old. Moreover, young people in general are not nearly as progressive as people think.—according to one poll, Gen Z—born mid-90s to 2010 or so——is less likely to support cancel culture than all other age groups.[84] I make a point of asking my kids' and stepkids' friends, who range in age from seventeen to twenty-five, about their political and social beliefs. While they're nearly all left of center, rarely are they hardcore ideologues. Most are critical of woke culture and poke fun at it—in the safety of their friends' circles. Yet Jewish organizations have largely essentialized the voices of young Jews, just as they have Jews of color. They then use this slice of the younger demographic to design programming for all with a decided Progressive political bent. As comedian Bill Maher quips, "The kids are running the asylum now."

A Case for Optimism?

After the November 2021 elections, in which Republican Glenn Youngkin defeated presumed frontrunner Democrat Terry McAuliffe for Virginia governor, I spoke again with Barry Shrage, this time about the encroachment of woke ideology on Jewish life. Shrage opposes the ideology in no uncertain terms: "Anti-racism does not represent a Jewish vision of a better world," he told me. Forever the optimist, Shrage was giddy about the election results in Virginia, Buffalo, and Minneapolis, which he viewed as a resounding defeat of woke ideology. Significant numbers of Virginians who voted for Joe Biden in 2020, more than half of whom were independent voters, went on in 2021 to vote for a Republican gubernatorial candidate who pledged to push back on critical race ideology. These voters saw the assignments their children brought home and overheard the Zoom classroom discussions, and were rightly horrified. "This will turn the tide," Shrage foretold.

A few months later, Shrage repeated this prediction in an interview we conducted: "The entire woke superstructure hit an iceberg in Virginia, I think it hit another iceberg in San Francisco," he stated,[85] referring to the Spring 2022 recall of three San Francisco Board of Education commissioners who had adopted extreme woke positions, and who were voted out of office by 70 percent of the voters. I shared Shrage's hope but not his optimism. If politics is downstream from culture, as the old saying goes, then institutional change is far, far downstream from politics. It would take more than a series of electoral defeats, I reckoned, to undo the juggernaut of identitarian deference—not only in Jewish organizations, but even in the Democratic party, which is supposedly in the business of winning elections. In March of 2022, I sat next to a Democratic operative from Virginia at a dinner in New York. Even in a private conversation, she would not acknowledge the manifest liability of woke politics to Democratic electoral success. "It's almost like Democrats are living in Mark Zuckerberg's Metaverse, an alternative reality that makes true believers feel good but is disconnected from the harsh reality in the real world," stated Josh Kraushaar, a Virginia-based political analyst and columnist for the *National Journal*.[86]

Doubling Down

In observing Jewish and other institutions over the past few years, I've noted three indicators of woke institutional capture. Any one of them probably tells you all you need to know. Indeed, where there's woke smoke there's probably more fire than anyone realizes. Dig deep enough, and you'll probably find all three indicators.

First, an act of identitarian deference, such as hiring a new DEI coordinator or team, and giving them total autonomous control over the organization's DEI efforts. Second, one or a series of mandatory DEI trainings that prescribe the one true way to understand race and racism in American society. These DEI programs can serve a ritualistic purpose—not unlike a Bar or Bat Mitzvah—of inscribing members into the fold. No one objects—no one is allowed to object—so everyone must be on board. Third, in all its public pronouncements and programming, the organization adheres to the one acceptable point of view on matters of race, racism, and social disparities. This third indicator is particularly conspicuous in Jewish public policy organizations with a tradition of debating controversial issues; they cease debating and pretend there's only one legitimate viewpoint and that the issues are settled in the public or Jewish mind, when, in fact, there isn't, and they aren't.

In March of 2022, I joined a Zoom talk hosted by Kol Shalom Congregation in Rockville, Maryland, a synagogue I attended for a while but did not join. The program was titled "School Boards Under Attack" and featured Shirley Brandman, a former chair of the Montgomery County Public Schools (MCPS) School Board, who spoke about what she described as the assault on school boards by angry parents. According to Brandman, many parents want to "prohibit educators from teaching or instructing or training on complex issues around race." (Brandman is now an education advocate serving as a strategic adviser to Montgomery County's Black and Brown Coalition for Educational Equity and

Excellence. A Yale Law grad, she is exceedingly well-spoken; I can see why she became chair of the Board of Education in a large county with a nearly $3 billion public education budget.) As evidence of the supposed epidemic of harassment by parents of school board members, Brandman cited a *Reuters* story that found 220 threatening or harassing emails sent by angry parents to school board members in a fifteen-state sampling.[87] This may sound like a lot—one is too many—but half of these emails were sent to one person in Loudoun County, Virginia. There are twenty-five school districts in Maryland alone. A hundred or so incendiary messages sent to upwards of four hundred school districts in Virginia is not exactly a national emergency. And *Reuters* didn't bother to count the messages that were entirely civil in tone while challenging proposed changes to school curriculum or mask mandates.

In Loudoun County, the epicenter of the educational culture war, a few parents did indeed show up to school board meetings very angry and went off the rails, shouting insults and veiled threats. But many more, like Emily Curtis, a Biden voter, simply expressed disagreement, finding it "deeply worrying that the school system is using terms such as white supremacy and systemic racism," which, she fears, "will trickle through to the classroom, dividing children into racial groups and teaching them that their race decides their fate."[88] Curtis' completely valid concerns about today's anti-racist education are being lumped in with the few radical activists who threaten school board members so as to discredit her and others with her views. The message from school officials is loud and clear: either accept the established view on anti-racism education, or we will smear you as a hatemonger.

I began to see other mainstream Jewish organizations repeat the same mantra about the attack on school boards and deny all legitimacy to the other side of the debate. In the Spring of 2022, the Jewish Council for Public Affairs (JCPA)—the organization I had headed—held a panel on "The Rise of Local Extremism" with five speakers. All addressed so-called "attacks" on school boards and the campaign against teaching CRT in the classroom. Not one of the speakers acknowledged that there was even another side to school board controversies or that parents might have a valid gripe about curriculum that school boards should at least acknowledge. Emily Kaufman, a researcher for the Anti-Defamation

League's Center on Extremism, stated that "[S]chool board meetings encountered...disinformation and conspiracies around critical race theory.... [W]e've seen extremists weaponize critical race theory to leverage their own conspiracies around white genocide." Shannon Saul of Keshet, a Jewish LGBT rights organization, said, "We've seen rhetoric emerging recently among extremists that is very similar to rhetoric that Jews have faced in the past for...teaching about the Holocaust or that racism is damaging to children." Dr. Tarece Johnson, Chair of Georgia's diverse Gwinnett County Schools, stated, "I am an outspoken person about CRT, however, as a school board member I also can say that we don't teach CRT in our school system, so the specific targeting that I have endured has really been because I do talk about systemic racism and structural racism." Dan Frankel, a Democratic member of the Pennsylvania House of Representatives, stated, "We had a bill that was going to require every school district to publish on the internet the entire curriculum...essentially opening up Pennsylvania's public schools to scrutiny from around the country from every lunatic group you can imagine." Representative Andy Schwartz, a Jewish legislator from Wyoming, railed against state-level anti-CRT bills, which he had a hand in killing in his state legislature.[89]

Whether or not one calls these changes to school curriculum CRT, they are certainly an outgrowth of CRT, and parents might view Dr. Johnson's position on teaching systemic and structural racism in the schools as teaching kids precisely what to think about race and racism while denying them the room to think for themselves. My own kids' school district in Montgomery County, Maryland, is undertaking an "anti-racist audit" that preliminarily recommends that students learn to "identify and resist systems of oppression." Given this effort to indoctrinate kids in woke ideology, is it any wonder parents want transparency in the curriculum—which one panelist, Dan Frankel, treats as a form of extremism? Judging from the agendas of these forums, rank and file Jews have not even heard an alternative perspective about the school curriculum debate.

In an Anti-Defamation League guide for parents, "Family Conversations about Current Events," titled, "What is Critical Race Theory and Why is It in the News So Much?" claims that "CRT helps us understand how laws and policies, even the ones that aren't explicitly about race or racism...can cause or worsen racial disparities. By focusing on laws, policies and systems, CRT helps us understand how and why racial injustice continues to persist in the US despite the progress that has been made towards racial equity."[90] Based on this reading alone, one might think that critical race *theory* isn't a theory at all but rather a dogma that the ADL endorses.

The ADL continues: "The term 'critical race theory' is being used in the media and in political campaigns to incite fear and misinform parents and the public. Yet, there is no evidence that critical race theory is being taught in K–12 schools. It is not a curriculum, a teaching practice or a typical area of study in teacher preparation." This despite many schools explicitly stating they are teaching CRT, and the National Education Association (NEA)—the nation's largest teacher's union—receiving approval and funding for a plan promoting CRT in K–12 curricula, in all fifty states.[91] The ADL further opines that CRT critics "assert their strong disagreement with the teaching of CRT despite being unable to define it or describe how it's being taught in schools. Some of these people have been influenced or swayed by misinformation." The authors of the ADL backgrounder, it appears, have themselves been swayed by misinformation. If the ADL bothered to showcase an alternative perspective from one of the numerous thoughtful critics of current racial pedagogy, they would likely hear quite a compelling critique of how race and racism are taught in many schools. At least then their members and the broader public could reach an informed understanding.

As a longtime admirer of the ADL—who appreciates the organization's work in combating antisemitism and racism, in tracking and cataloging extremism and hate crimes, and in training law enforcement—I am pained to see this particular organization embrace woke ideology without any sense of how it fuels antisemitism and illiberalism. CEO Jonathan Greenblatt recently warned about the threat of antisemitism on the political left, aptly comparing it to "climate change" in his various writings. But the ADL's work in the education sphere shows that the venerable organization has yet to grasp the ideological wellspring of Progressive antisemitism. In an ADL guide called "How Should I Talk About Race in My Mostly White Classroom?", teachers are instructed to "define white privilege as: 'unearned and often unseen or unrecognized advantages, benefits or rights conferred upon people based on their membership in a dominant group (e.g. white people, heterosexual people, men, able-bodied, etc.).'"[92] The organization must not simultaneously argue for a fixed hierarchy of privilege in society with whites at the top, while it fights antisemitism that emanates from malevolent activists who insist that Jews are white and at the very pinnacle of power, oppressing other minorities. The ADL seems to have entirely missed the obvious connection between the spread of illiberal ideology on the left and the growth of a new variant of Progressive antisemitism that insists that Jews are all-powerful and oppressive.

In a forum held in August 2021 called "Disrupting Bias in Education," the ADL's director of curriculum and training stated, "We also need to understand the relationship between our identity and bias and power. So within societal systems, some social identities have more access to power and privilege, and some are marginalized."[93] Insisting that there is a fixed relationship between "identity and bias and power" legitimizes and encourages bad actors to assert a relationship between Jewish identity and power—a classical antisemitic trope. Well-meaning though they may be, such assertions coming from ADL professionals inevitably fuel notions of Jewish power and privilege. Unless and until the ADL stops insisting on a rigid hierarchy of privilege and power, the organization will be fighting on both sides of the war on antisemitism. (As this book neared publication, the ADL announced that it was undertaking a review of its educational materials. "We are far from perfect and clearly there is content among our curricular materials that is misaligned with ADL's values and strategy. We intend to address this issue immediately and openly. We are moving to launch a thorough review of our education content," it stated. This is an excellent first step.)

The Union for Reform Judaism (URJ) has gone even further down the ideological rabbit hole. In the Spring of 2022, the Religious Action Center of Reform Judaism offered a four-part course for rabbis and cantors to "learn" race and racism. "Together," the URJ proclaimed of this diversity training, "we will explore the ways we are affected by antisemitism and consider how we simultaneously benefit from the same systems of oppression we are trying to dismantle. This series will help us to deepen our commitment to and capacity for leveraging our position as white antiracists and support the work of creating multiracial, multicultural communities where Jews of all backgrounds can experience belonging. This space," the URJ explained, "is for white clergy and will serve as a white antiracist affinity space. A white antiracist affinity space is one where white people can process their emotions and deepen their understanding around race and racism, without burdening or causing additional harm to People of Color (POC)." The URJ education program was designed to help rabbis "better understand our own identities as white Jews," "learn how to recognize the invisibility of 'whiteness' (including patriarchal, heteronormative, Puritan/Christian values) that have become normalized," and "understand how to disrupt our daily acts of 'whiteness' (behaviors and actions we may perpetuate unknowingly as they have been adapted overtime and deemed 'the standard' but may or may not be useful to our efforts towards creating communities of belonging)."[94]

Imagine the preaching from the pulpit that will come out of such training, the Sunday school lesson plans, the fireside indoctrination at summer camps, and the youth group activities fostered by graduates of "white anti-racist affinity groups," by rabbis who will teach Jews to "disrupt…daily acts of whiteness." The Reform Movement's embrace of radical forms of DEI demonstrates a central point in my argument here: embracing dogma inevitably leads to embracing ever more extreme forms of that dogma. Undoubtedly, the denomination's earlier forms of diversity training, if any, didn't involve placing rabbis in white affinity groups and confessing to their complicity in whiteness. Such lunacy doesn't happen overnight. People need time to accept new dogma as truth, to defer to new leaders for moral authority, to insist that everyone in their ranks buy into the dogma, then to keep up with new iterations of the ideology, no matter how absurd or pernicious they become. What will Reform Judaism look like five or ten years down the road? One can hope that more rabbis will oppose this ideological onslaught, as a segment did in the Rabbis' Letter I mentioned earlier. Unless more Reform Jews speak up, woke ideology will define the Reform denomination and a vast swath of American Jewish life for years to come.

Sadly, Jewish day schools and other educational institutions have also adopted such programs, teaching Jewish students how they "benefit from systems of oppression." The DEI student resource page of the Charles E. Smith Jewish Day School—taken down after parents intervened—featured a *Forward* article by Nylah Burton called "White Jews: Stop Calling Yourselves 'White-Passing,'" in which Burton stated, "I strongly feel that de-assimilation and the dismantling of whiteness is critical to both the eradication of racism and the survival of the Jewish people."[95] The student resource page offered several similarly themed articles but omitted any critique or alternative perspective whatsoever for the students' consideration. In the fall of 2021, the JILV conducted a national scan of pluralistic Jewish day schools like Charles E. Smith, and found that the vast majority of the forty-five schools had taken steps to embrace DEI. Some, but not all, had student resource pages like Charles E. Smith's, with no alternative viewpoint in sight.

Like the participants in the forums on school boards, ADL educational programs, and the Reform movement's white affinity groups, today's Jewish students are hearing only one side of the issues. They are taught to dismiss millions of Americans who look at the issues differently, without so much as wondering where the differers get their ideas. Jewish organizations hitherto known for their openness to varied points of view, disputatiousness, and commitment to critical thinking, have taken the leap of faith into identitarian deference. They've ended the debate. The only thing left to do is share the good news with an ever-growing percentage of their minions (and minyans). They don't realize that they've signed up for an ideology that is guaranteed to foment antisemitism. Ironically, Jewish woke adherents *are* complicit—not in white supremacy, but in unilaterally disarming the Jewish community in the fight against antisemitism and sapping the community's resolve.

CHAPTER 10

FUELING ANTISEMITISM

Cause or Effect?

Is woke ideology *inherently* antisemitic? You may be surprised to know that I don't think it is. There is nothing inherently antisemitic about, for example, linking identity to privilege. But there is plenty of dogma in doing so when, for example, proponents insist that being white and male automatically bestows advantage in every context while being Black and female likewise automatically confers disadvantage. Sometimes, those immutable characteristics are, as claimed, advantages or disadvantages. Sometimes, however, a supposed disadvantage can become an advantage, and vice versa. Often, in life's varied circumstances, such identities make little difference whatsoever. It's both dogmatic and dangerous to insist that identity is a proxy for oppression and privilege, and to bully others into acquiescence, thereby creating an opportunity for more radical actors—the haters, who are always looking for an excuse—to make a more radical claim linking Jewish identity to privilege.

Moreover, Jews fare better in open, liberal environments, and less well in closed, illiberal environments. According to the writer Dara Horn, "Since ancient times, in every place they have ever lived, Jews have represented the frightening prospect of freedom. As long as Jews existed in any society, there was evidence that it in fact wasn't necessary to believe what everyone else believed, that those who disagreed with their neighbors could survive and even flourish against all odds."[96] A society that begins to make it harder for people to express their beliefs is an ominous indicator that the society could turn on its Jews. There is nothing inherent about illiberalism spawning antisemitism, but there is—given Jewish history—something inevitable about it. Linking identity to privilege doesn't automatically lead to linking Jewish identity to "Jewish privilege," but that is where such linkages invariably end up: Jewish privilege is a mere half-step from white privilege.

British-born writer Andrew Sullivan similarly points out that vilifying "whiteness" leads to vilifying Jews. "If you replace the word 'whiteness' with 'Jewishness,'" Sullivan says, "this kind of demonizing rhetoric could be straight from a Nazi textbook. It identifies a racial group, it attaches evil characteristics to it, it ascribes those characteristics to individuals within that group, and it sees their success as won at the direct expense of others. The logic of anti-whiteness and anti-Semitism blur, over time, into the same thing."[97] Bishop Talbert Swan, a prominent Christian religious figure and a local NAACP President, tweeted on May 2022, "Whiteness is an unrelenting, demonic force of evil." Unacceptable in its demonization of whiteness, it's very easy to see how this rhetoric could be applied to Jews, a vulnerable minority group. And inasmuch as Jews are perceived as white, it already does. The disparagement of whites doesn't have to lead to the disparagement of Jews, but Sullivan is nevertheless correct that this connection has begun to be made and will likely continue in the future.

There is a reason people make such connections so readily. Even when antisemitism is pushed to the margins of society—held in check by seemingly sturdy guardrails of public discourse—it's never far from public view. For thousands of years, the same conspiracy theories, the same disdain, and the same impulse to scapegoat has coursed through Western and non-Western societies alike. Deborah Lipstadt states, "[T]hough its outer form may evolve over time, its essence remains the same. It's not unlike a stubborn infection. Medication may alleviate the symptoms, but the infection itself lies dormant and may reemerge at an opportune moment in a new incarnation."[98] And when the guardrails of public discourse begin to wobble, when the terms of discussion change and create an opening—a permission structure—antisemitism can come back with a roar. In the name of "justice," woke ideology provides just such a permission structure by legitimizing portrayals of people who can be—and are, and will be—targeted by others looking for excuses to spread hate. That's why it's so disheartening to watch Jewish organizations that should know better—and in some cases, do know better—pay tribute to the very ideological tendencies that activate latent antisemitic tropes.

The Oppressor vs. The Oppressed

If there was one moment when many American Jews realized that we might have a problem with woke ideology, it was in May 2021, when fighting broke out in Gaza between Israel and Iran-backed Hamas. I have studied media coverage of that ongoing conflict since it first broke out in June 2008, and of each subsequent conflict: December 2008, November 2012, June 2014, and May 2018. Up until recently, media coverage—both news and opinion—unfolded in a predictable pattern: the stories and editorials acknowledged that Israel must have leeway to defend itself against Hamas rocket fire aimed at Israeli civilians. Then, as casualties mounted, the coverage turned against Israel, and within a few days, the same outlets lambasted the Jewish state for using "disproportionate force." In May 2021—when this latest round occurred—even in the earliest stages of the conflict, Israel was not given the usual benefit of the doubt and was demonized as the oppressor in some quarters.

The social media was even worse. "If you've been paying attention to social media over the past week, you will have seen this same attempt to redefine the Israeli-Palestinian conflict as a racial power dynamic, casting Israel as infinitely powerful and Palestinians as completely without agency," Batya Ungar-Sargon pointed out in a *Newsweek* editorial, "When Wokeness Comes for Israel," in May 2021. "It certainly makes for worse Instagram posts. 'Israelis are the OPPRESSORS and Palestinians are the OPPRESSED,' one viral Instagram post reads. 'There is no "fighting," there is only Israeli colonisation, ethnic cleansing, military occupation, and apartheid.'"[99]

What changed in this latest round? Certainly not the conditions on the ground in the Middle East. A close look at nearly every bout of fighting reveals that Hamas' leadership needed a violent escalation to stay in power in the face of an increasingly disgruntled Gaza population and civil service. What changed was the ideological environment in the US—namely, the ascendance of woke ideology. "What's new," states Ungar-Sargon, "is the ubiquity of such (woke) discourse in mainstream American media. In the past, we didn't see 'Israel's Colonialist Project' in *Washington Post* headlines, nor did MSNBC insist that 'The latest Israel-Palestine crisis isn't a "real estate dispute." It's ethnic cleansing.'" Ungar-Sargon continues, "Wokeness is a poor enough lens for understanding our own problems here in the U.S. Its distortions are even worse when it comes to the Middle East."

In an August 2021 article in *The Daily Beast*, reporter Tirhakah Love went on an anti-Zionist rant at the announcement that the game-show Jeopardy would be hosted by Mayim Bialik, a proud Jewish actor. "Speaking of gods and shady behavior," stated Love, "Bialik loudly proclaimed her donation toward bulletproof vests for the genocidal Israeli Defense Forces back in 2014 just out of 'a need to do something.' After facing backlash, she quieted for a time until May of this year, where she self-identified as a 'liberal Zionist' who, like many other celebrities, spouted bothsidesism." Love also said in a Tweet that Zionism is "a faux ethno-religious liberation movement that is staunchly imperialistic as it's an extension of British colonialism and an articulation of white supremacy."[100] "White supremacy" applied to the Israel-Palestinian conflict? Where have I heard that term before?

Oppressor v. Oppressed is always the default orientation of the woke left, whose ideologues equate power with depravity and powerlessness with virtue. Through this bifurcated lens, the "weak" Palestinians are the perennial victims, and the "strong" Israelis are the perennial victimizers, with no room anywhere for nuance of any kind. Some woke Progressives go further and see successful Jews as oppressors of other minorities and even of poor whites, shading into rightwing antisemitism of the type generated by the KKK. Thus does an ideology that consists of simplistic thinking lend itself to simplistic thinking about Jews and Israel.

Defining Jews as White

Nicole Levitt is a staff attorney for Women Against Abuse (WAA), an organization that supports women experiencing domestic violence in

Philadelphia, Pennsylvania. She defends domestic violence victims in court, loves her job, and is deeply committed to her clients. Nicole is also an Orthodox Jew whose primary identity is Jewish. Like many organizations in its sector, WAA went through a DEI process in the immediate aftermath of the George Floyd murder in response to the "violence, erasure, and racism currently being levied at the Black community in the United States."

Employees of the WAA legal center—Nicole among them—were divided by race and forced into affinity groups, with the white group directed to focus on anti-racist ideology. According to a complaint filed with the Equal Employment Opportunities Commission (EEOC), activities in these racially segregated groups mandated sharing "with vulnerability and honesty" as coworkers "unpack how and where AntiBlackness showed up in childhood, young adulthood, and how it manifests today." Groups were asked to engage in sharing "positive," "negative," "current," and "past memories of whiteness and white people," and "blackness and black people." The White affinity group was asked to sign a contract stating they "[o]wn that all white people are racist and I am not the exception."[101]

The contract was Nicole's last straw. When she refused to sign, she was required to write a definition of "allyship" to present to the Black Affinity Group. The WAA claimed that because it is based in a large city and serves many Black clients, all of its employees needed to do this work to make Black and Brown clients feel safe. The implied threat was that if a WAA employee didn't agree with the anti-racist ideology, they were making WAA clients feel unsafe, and hence disqualifying themselves as their professional advocates.

"At first I wasn't going to speak out," said Levitt. "I thought I would just kind of ride it out. But it became so egregious that I felt that I couldn't keep my integrity and not say anything. And I realized there's going to be a price to pay. And there was. And there probably still is but there's also a price to pay by not speaking out." Levitt decided to initiate legal proceedings. "As a Jew the racial concept of black vs. white was irrelevant. I've never considered myself in those terms, and I didn't want to take part in an exercise that demanded it." The WAA's diversity program would force an employee to adopt an identity she didn't have.[102]

The Reut Group—an Israeli think tank that closely monitors and analyzes ideological trends in the US—popularized the term "erasive anti-Semitism" in March 2021, referring to "a *de-facto* undermining of the Jewish narrative of self-determination." According to Reut, erasive anti-Semitism negates the rights of Jews—individually or collectively—to define their identity, experience, and vulnerability. Reut regards it as largely an "unintended consequence of contemporary progressive discourse," and argues that current Progressive discourse distorts the historic and lived experience of Jews, who are "cast uniformly as powerful white oppressors." Unlike other forms of discrimination, according to Reut, this strain of woke ideology does not single out Jews. Rather, it indiscriminately lumps them within the dominant majority. This effectively erases the Jewish voice in defining Jewish identity. Reut points out: "There is a marginal fringe that purposefully advances anti-Jewish and anti-Israel agendas utilizing its tenets and continues to amass influence on the left."[103]

In a powerful article in *Sapir* in Spring 2021, Pamela Paresky wrote, "Race is the locus of power in the critical social justice worldview, which holds that the dominant group—white people—will, when it serves their interests, conditionally invite minority groups into 'whiteness.'" According to this paradigm, light-skinned Jews can benefit from whiteness by shedding Jewish ethnic markers and are thus granted "conditional whiteness." Paresky states that "Jews, who have never been seen as white by those for whom being white is a moral good, are now seen as white by those for whom whiteness is an unmitigated evil. This reflects the nature of antisemitism: No matter the grievance or the identity of the aggrieved, Jews are held responsible. Critical race theory does not merely make it easy to demonize Jews using the language of social justice; it makes it difficult not to."[104]

Indeed, the idea has gained ground in woke ideological circles that Jews (with the exceptions of those who qualify as people of color) are "white adjacent," should properly be regarded as white, and must accept their whiteness. In a January 2021 episode of the TV program *The View*, Whoopi Goldberg stated that the Holocaust was about "man's inhumanity to man" and "not about race." When one of her co-hosts challenged her, arguing that the Holocaust was driven by white supremacy, Goldberg replied, “But these are two white groups of people.” She added, “This is white people doing it to white people, so y’all going to fight amongst yourselves.” A day later, on *The Late Show with Stephen Colbert*, she doubled down, calling the Holocaust “white-on-white” crime—a grotesque depiction often made by hardened antisemites. Goldberg was suspended from the show for two weeks.[105]

While there’s no reason to believe that Goldberg harbors ill will toward Jewish people, this sordid affair demonstrates how the whiteness/people of color binary can be turned into an anti-Jewish canard. In May 2020, Gazi Kodzo, a radical Black social media influencer, described Anne Frank as a “Becky,”[106] a stereotype of a white woman who leverages her privilege. His contention is that the story of Anne Frank is taught in schools while genocide against Black people and people of color have been largely ignored. “Genocide wasn’t even a WORD until the WHITE ON WHITE of the Holocaust,” Kodzo tweeted. When in July 2022 Slate editor Jordan Weissman tweeted out “‘Anne Frank had white privilege’ feels like a nail in the coffin for a certain kind of discourse,” prominent *New York Times* writer Nicole Hannah Jones responded, “I mean, what kind of discourse would you categorize this as outside of fringe, ignorant and ridiculous? Serious question: What type of discourse?”[107] Numerous Jewish progressives endorsed her comments, dismissing such vulgarities as outliers. And, of course, the vast majority of woke people would never dream of portraying Anne Frank in such a manner. But here’s the thing about ideology: it continually outdoes itself and spawns more radical claims.

"Jewish Privilege"

In July 2020, #JewishPrivilege trended on Twitter, meaning that it was among the most popular phrases on the social media site. “White nationalists had created the hashtag to spread anti-Semitic conspiracies about Jews being ‘privileged’—that we control the media, the banks and the world,” stated Hen Mazzig, an Israeli-born writer and Fellow at the Tel Aviv Institute. Soon after, Mazzig recounts, Progressive voices joined the fray, perhaps because the term “Jewish privilege” sounded similar to “white privilege.” The ensuing Twitter mob claimed that Jews are not a target of hate or bias, but are responsible for the oppression perpetrated against other minorities.[108]

Mazzig continued, "Apparently seeking to lure progressives into their anti-Semitic vortex, these nameless online shadows instructed activists to use quotes from 'Malcolm, Farrakhan and Mandela about Jews,' 'to include BLM [Black Lives Matter] related hashtags,' and 'to promote the conspiracy theory that Jews funded the slave trade (often promoted by Farrakhan and the Nation of Islam) and are behind racism in America.'" In order to refute the #JewishPrivilege libel, Mazzig urged Jews to share their personal stories of antisemitism on Twitter. Within a few hours, the hashtag was coopted by hundreds of Jews sharing their experiences of hatred and discrimination. Celebrities, such as Sarah Silverman and David Baddiel, chimed in with their own experiences.

This was by no means the first time "Jewish privilege" popped up in the public square: it had been circulating in the cultural ether for several years by the time #JewishPrivilege appeared. In April 2016, a debate erupted in the Stanford University Senate over a resolution condemning antisemitism. The controversy revolved around comments made by a student senator who denied it was antisemitic to claim Jews control the media, banks, etc. Lost in the outcry was a supposedly less blatant canard offered up by other students that "some stressed the importance of understanding the intersection of 'white power' and 'Jewish power' before voting on the resolution," reported the *Stanford Review*.[109] In other words, it was not ok to use the rightwing, white supremacist idiom naming specific institutions that Jews supposedly control, but it was ok to use the progressive idiom making strikingly similar claims. One can see how a slight change in language allows antisemites to say roughly the same thing.

In March of 2017, antisemitic fliers calling for an end to "Jewish privilege" were posted all over campus at the University of Illinois at Chicago. "Ending white privilege starts with ending Jewish privilege," the flier proclaimed. It falsely stated that "forty-four percent of American Jews are in the top 1% of income earners." Mazzig and others may have successfully stemmed the tide on Twitter in that one instance, but the connection between "Jewish" and "privilege" is nevertheless etched into the neural pathways of the public mind and will remain so as long as the idea of linking identity to privilege holds cultural currency.

Survey data shows a strong correlation between woke political attitudes and antisemitism on the left. The Jewish Institute for Liberal Values commissioned a poll conducted from July 30–August 3, 2022 consisting of 1,600 likely voters (margin of error +/- 2.5 percent). Survey respondents were split roughly between Democratic and Republican voters. Among questions respondents were asked was: "Do you agree or disagree with the following statement? America is a structurally racist country in which white Americans, and white-adjacent groups who emulate white culture (like Asian Americans and Jewish Americans), have unfair advantages over minorities which must be addressed to achieve equity?" The poll revealed (shown below) that those on the far left were much more likely to agree with the statement, a clear indication that woke ideological attitudes about structural racism are fueling antisemitic and anti-Asian sentiment (viewing Jews and Asians as privileged).

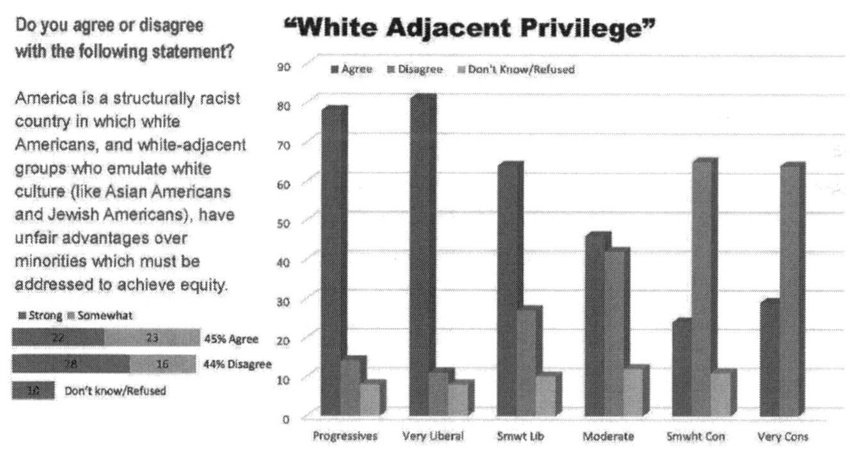

Poll conducted by OnMessage Public Strategies.

Shockingly, some Progressive Jews have used the term "Jewish privilege" in the same way antisemites use it. In an August 2017 opinion piece in the *Washington Post*, prominent rabbi and author Danya Ruttenberg stated, "So here's the paradox: Anti-Semitism and Jewish privilege are, and have long been, two sides of the same coin. On the one hand, Jews as a category are thus far shielded from the state violence that a lot of other groups are experiencing.... Although of course there are Jews of all levels of economic security in this country, American Jews as a collective do have a lot more social and cultural capital than many other groups, and we are not as vulnerable as other communities under attack."[110] The term "Jewish privilege" does not imply that Jews on average have done well in American society. If that's the standard, then what's next? "Asian American privilege"? or "Nigerian American privilege" (among the most successful immigrant groups)?

The term "Jewish privilege" implies that just by being Jewish (as opposed to being perceived as white) one obtains certain benefits in a white supremacist society. This is both absurd and outrageous, not to mention dangerous to Jews. In an August 2020 article in the *Atlanta Jewish Times*, "What is 'Jewish Privilege?' It's Complicated," journalist Dave Schechter explores whether the notion of Jewish privilege has any legitimacy. When Schechter put this question to Tarece Johnson, Georgia-based school board chair and Jew of color, Johnson answered, "No. There is White privilege, and some Jews who happen to be White or White-passing benefit from living in a racist and anti-Black society.... Antisemitism is not a benefit and it is certainly not a privilege to experience hate because of your religion, ancestry, and/or culture. So, in my opinion, being Jewish is not a 'privilege,' in the racialized social meaning of the word, but being White may certainly afford opportunities that non-White people just are not privileged to experience." Schechter ends his article with "So, are Jews privileged? It's complicated."[111]

No, it's really not complicated at all. The answer is no. Jews—and everyone else—should stop pouring fuel on this highly combustible antisemitic distortion.

Jews and "Equity"

What could possibly be wrong with a term that sounds as benevolent as "equity"? Ibram X. Kendi defined the term in his best seller *How to be an Antiracist*: "Racial inequity is when two or more racial groups are not standing on approximately equal footing." Discrimination that produces equity, Kendi assures us, is anti-racist. At first blush, this may sound like a fine approach to leveling the playing field.[112] But think through the consequences and you'll see how radical a departure it is from our traditional understanding of "equality," when it becomes clear that not only is this view of equity bad for society, it's detrimental to Jewish wellbeing.

In May 2021, Anna Keating, who had just quit her job in the chaplaincy services for Colorado College, wrote an essay for the *Hedgehog Review* in which she described how the concept of equity played out at her former place of employment: "[The] administrator decided that because Jews, being a tiny percentage of the US population, are overrepresented in higher education generally, and at the college where I worked in particular, antiracism in this instance required that the number of Jewish students be reduced." In addition to reducing its Jewish population, Keating said that the school wanted to eliminate Jewish religious practice. She quoted her supervisor: "Because of the college's commitment to antiracism and equity the question finally becomes, Is chaplaincy sustainable? Our Jewish community has the support of its alumni donor. How do we manage that? And Roman Catholic students and others interested in Catholicism can apply for grants from an endowed fund for Roman Catholic Studies. And in order to be antiracist we have to have equal resources for Hindu students, Muslim students, Buddhist students, or we need to do away with Spiritual Life groups all together." Keating explained, "[B]ecause there were 60 students at Shabbat and only a handful of Muslim students on campus, the Jewish group should not exist."[113]

In other words, if you can't find enough people from the disadvantaged group to achieve proportional representation (with no real pipeline in place, how can you?) then you must reduce the numbers of the advantaged group. Just imagine if this idea were brought to scale in all the places where Jews are overrepresented—academia, business, science, medicine, law, etc.—and all the places they would need to be, well, purged. "This obviously presents a particular problem for Jews, who represent roughly 2 percent of the U.S. population," stated Pamela Paresky. "A much higher proportion of Jews than non-Jews attend college. Jews represent an outsize share of winners of major awards, like Nobel prizes.

As of 2020, seven of the 20 wealthiest Americans were Jewish. In virtually every major American industry and institution, Jews hold leadership roles disproportionate to their overall demographic numbers."[114]

Moreover, according to noted Black economist at Brown University, Glenn Loury—in a May 2021 discussion with Bari Weiss titled "Anti-Racism and Anti-Semitism Collide"—the notion of equity can generate resentment against successful groups. Loury stated that "One consequence of a fixation on group disparities understood to be the necessary consequence of oppression or racism is that the groups that do well will come under suspicion. Their success will be thought to be the flip side of the disadvantage of the groups that do poorly. If African Americans are underrepresented in this or that venue because of systemic racism, and Jews are let's say overrepresented in those very same venues, how can it be otherwise but that the over-representation of the Jews is somehow the bitter fruit, the necessary consequence of that very system of oppression that excludes African Americans?.... That de-legitimation of the success of groups that do well is very very dangerous. It strikes me that it does fuel resentment and envy and a kind of antipathy that can easily express itself in violence."

Well before Ibram X. Kendi entered the scene and bequeathed us his version of "equity," scholars could foresee how such a concept, emerging out of the Critical Race scholarship of the time, would encourage antisemitism. In a chapter in their 1995 book, *Beyond All Reason: The Radical Assault on Truth in American Law*,[115] "Is the Radical Critique of Merit Antisemitic," legal scholars Daniel Farber and Suzanna Sherry well understood the threat:

> Conventional concepts of merit are under attack by some Critical Legal Scholars, Critical Race Theorists, and radical feminists. These critics contend that "merit" is only a social construct designed to maintain the power of dominant groups. This Article challenges the reductionist view that merit has no meaning except as a tool for those in power to perpetuate the existing social order. The authors observe that certain traditionally oppressed groups, most notably Jews and Asian Americans, are

> disproportionately represented in some desirable economic and educational positions. They have in that sense "succeeded" beyond the supposedly dominant majority. The economic and educational accomplishments of these groups are hard to reconcile with the notion that "merit" exists solely to perpetuate the power of the dominant majority (white Gentiles). Because the radical critique of merit denies that the accomplishments of these minority groups can be explained by genuine merit, it necessarily implies that these groups have obtained an unfair proportion of desirable social goods. Therefore, the authors suggest, the radical critique of merit has the wholly unintended consequence of being anti-Semitic and possibly racist.

The link between this ideology, particularly the Kendi understanding of equity, and the growth of antisemitism was not only foreseeable, but it was also foreseen. Have Jewish organizations that have lined up behind this dangerous version of equity really thought this one through?

Decentering Jews and Antisemitism

In June of 2021, two Jewish mental health providers at Stanford University alleged they were the targets of anti-Jewish harassment. Ron Albucher, a prominent psychiatrist, and Sheila Levin, a clinical social worker, filed a complaint with the EEOC alleging that Stanford University's Counseling & Psychological Services' DEI program had become a hostile environment for Jews.

In May 2020, after a virtual town hall at Stanford was "Zoombombed" with racist messages, swastikas, and the N-word, the DEI committee raised the incident for discussion but, in order to keep the spotlight on anti-Black racism, declined to address the explicit antisemitism of the attack. Instead of acknowledging the incident as a danger to Jews, participants "accused Dr. Albucher of derailing the program's focus on anti-Black racism merely by raising the issue of antisemitism."

Two months later, swastikas were discovered inside a Stanford church, and the DEI program once again took a pass rather than discuss the incident's impact on Jews. "I did not feel in the least bit safe saying anything at all," Levin reported. "I feel terrible about it, but I actually watched as staff just tore Ron up just for asking why they omitted swastikas from the discussion.... They were talking about his privilege and that he was basically wanting to take up time talking about antisemitism, rather than focusing on anti-Black racism, which really wasn't true." So Albucher and Levin were forbidden to call an explicitly antisemitic act by its name, let alone devote group time to it, in favor of "centering Blackness," which—as we see here—can mean downplaying or even ignoring Jews and antisemitism.[116] The aforementioned case of Nicole Levitt also exhibited this tendency to dismiss antisemitism as a full-fledged Progressive concern.[117] When another Jewish staffer at the domestic violence nonprofit shared an article during DEI discussions about antisemitism in the Black Lives Matter movement, Levitt endorsed the article, responding to the rise in anti-Semitic violence, "I hope as an organization we would stand against this as well." Her email evoked numerous harsh responses, one of which called it "a slap in the face of every brown and black person." Antisemitism "is not woven into the fabric of American society," stated another staffer. "Whatever fear Jews feel," the staffer added, is "nothing compared to what black Americans feel."

Ben M. Freeman, author of the 2021 book *Jewish Pride*, made the point, "One crucial aspect of the Jewish experience today is that these specific framings of Jews as an all-powerful group make it difficult for some, particularly on the left, to recognize and address antisemitism. Because they perceive Jews to be powerful and privileged, it also shaped the manner those on the left express their own antisemitism. In other words, antisemitism 'punches up'—Jews are hated for their perceived power." In October 2020, Natalie Hopkinson, a professor of communications at Howard University, wrote an article in *The New York Times*, "The Women behind the Million Man March," which included a glowing portrayal of Minister Louis Farrakhan.[118] When readers called her out for her failure to address Farrakhan's grievous antisemitism, she replied on Twitter, "You know what makes me sad? Literally a million people involved in this essay. You don't center the marchers. You don't center the Black women who are named and linked. You don't even center

Farrakhan. You center yourself and your feelings."[119] As Hopkinson uses "centering," she demotes resistance to antisemitism to a selfish whine. She weaponizes one narrative to decenter another—an ironic move because anti-racist ideology purports to be "intersectional," to affirm the ways various forms of oppression interact with each other and amplify victimization. When it is used to shut down any other assertion of bigotry or hate, the centering/decentering paradigm elevates one form of bigotry above all else, neutralizing the very premise of intersectionality. That decentering has superseded intersectionality demonstrates how woke dogma can become more extreme and exclusionary over time.

In June 2020, the actor Jenny Slate left the cast of Netflix's highly popular *Big Mouth* because, she said, playing a half-Black, half-Jewish character as a white woman is "an act of erasure of Black people." She stated, "At the start of the show, I reasoned with myself that it was permissible for me to play 'Missy' because her mom is Jewish and White—as am I. But 'Missy' is also Black, and Black characters on an animated show should be played by Black people." Co-creators of the show said they agree with Slate's decision and apologized for casting a white person to voice a biracial character. "We made a mistake, took our privilege for granted, and we're working hard to do better moving forward," stated Nick Kroll, Andrew Goldberg, Mark Levin and Jennifer Flackett. Slate was replaced by Black actress, Ayo Edebiri. In this conception, it is wrong for an actor to be placed into a narrative that is not their own. Actor Kristen Bell, who similarly vacated her position on *South Park*, stated "Casting a mixed race character w/a white actress undermines the specificity of the mixed race & Black American experience."[120] Leaving aside the larger question about whether actors should be able to play characters of other identity groups (with a few exceptions, I have no problem with it at all), why is it acceptable for a Black person to voice a Jewish-Black character but not a Jewish person? How is such a prohibition not erasure of the Jewish person? This suggests that the Jewish experience and therefore Jewish characters do not enjoy the same sanctity—earned, apparently, through experience of oppression—as those of people of color. The Jewish narrative is thus de-centered.

The ascendency of the centering/decentering paradigm reverberates throughout society and downgrades antisemitism in the public mind. The hate-monitoring group the Southern Poverty Law Center (SPLC) recently ended the practice of monitoring Black radical antisemitism as a specific category. In an October 2020 announcement, "Equity Through Accuracy: Changes to Our Hate Map," SPLC stated, "In pursuit of a more accurate and more just hate map, the Intelligence Project (IP) (a department of SPLC) has committed to collapsing the Black Separatist listing. We will still monitor these groups, but we will be transferring them to hate ideologies, including antisemitism, that better describe the harm their rhetoric inflicts." The SPLC justified de-listing antisemitism from radical Black groups by pointing out "the common language shared by our Black Separatist listing and federal attempts to criminalize Black activism." SPLC further stated that "We reject federal law enforcement's false and misleading contention regarding threats from Black separatists.... These groups are very much part of activist spaces.... [T]he SPLC does not believe criminalizing and over-policing is an acceptable solution.... Yes, some Black nationalists have committed violence against Jewish communities, but those are fueled by antisemitism, not separatism."[121]

Here SPLC commits a similar conceptual error, as numerous Jewish organizations do, by denying any connection between Black separatist ideology and the antisemitism these radical forces trade in. Jew hatred is nearly always—explicitly or implicitly—a key feature of extremist, anti-democratic separatist belief systems. The SPLC wants to end law enforcement scrutiny of radical Black groups and individuals, some of whom have committed hate crimes against Jews, including the horrific December 2019 shooting spree in a Jersey City kosher grocery by a radical group calling themselves Black Hebrews. That these radical groups are integrated into "activist spaces" should not be taken as a sign that they are legitimate voices for social change, but that the activist spaces are willing to make common cause with radicals and tolerate their antisemitism. In short, in "centering" Black narratives of justice, the SPLC felt compelled to decenter a specific category of antisemitism coming from radical Black activists, thus raising the risks for Jews. In this woke construction, not only is antisemitism downgraded, not only is it driven out of the anti-racist conversation, but it also leaves Jewish communities vulnerable by stripping hate monitoring groups and law enforcement agencies—to the degree they take heed—of the capacity to fight Jew-hatred when it comes from Black extremist groups that are "very much part of activist spaces."

The (Still) Missing Link

The American Jewish community must recognize this variant of antisemitism's ideological roots in order to mobilize effective opposition. It's not enough to call out individual acts of Progressive antisemitism. Judging by current mainstream Jewish discourse, anyone might think that Progressive antisemitism mysteriously landed from outer space one day during The Great Racial Awakening. (I addressed this disconnect between symptom and cause of antisemitism earlier, when the Jewish community decried the ghastly chauvinism at the international assembly in Durban without any reference whatsoever to the postcolonial ideology at its root.) The ADL, for example, can cite chapter and verse of white nationalist ideology that foments antisemitism but cannot seem to muster the same analytical rigor to identify the ideological basis of left-wing antisemitism. When it analyzes alt-right antisemitism, the ADL states: "Alt right adherents identify with a range of different ideologies, all of which center on white identity. Many claim to be Identitarians, [who] espouse racism and intolerance under the guise of preserving the ethnic and cultural origins of their respective counties."[122] From this description, we get a clear sense of the ideology that animates this alt-right variant of antisemitism.

By contrast, in an October 2021 opinion piece in the *Washington Post* highlighting the dangers of Progressive antisemitism, ADL chief Jonathan Greenblatt asked, "What does it mean when the litmus test for inclusion in social justice spaces requires Jews to oppose the very existence of the only Jewish state in the world?"[123] In an otherwise exemplary editorial, Greenblatt neglects to address the ideological wellsprings that give rise to such bigoted tests. Jewish Progressive activist Isaac Luria goes much further and completely denies the existence of this form of antisemitism: in "Why Addressing Antisemitism Requires Fighting for Justice" in the Spring 2022 edition of the journal *Sources*, Luria implores the Jewish community to "Challenge the Jewish voices that charge racial and economic justice movements with spurious accusations of antisemitism."[124] This inability to acknowledge woke antisemitism and its impact on American Jews is an enduring blind spot in the American Jewish community. No wonder: many Jewish leaders are countenancing and, in some cases, are peddling the very ideology that foments Progressive antisemitism.

CHAPTER 11

DISENFRANCHISING AMERICAN JEWS

The Long View

Having explained how certain woke concepts create a new permission structure for antisemitism, I will now discuss the broader impact that woke antisemitism might have on Jewish life over time, and how this ideology could disenfranchise wide swaths of the American Jewish community and fundamentally compromise Jewish interests on the American scene.

When I think about the potential damage of woke ideology, I don't only think about what's happening now. I think about the damage that years of unchecked pandering to woke dogma could set afoot: how, over time, woke ideology could fundamentally alter our social architecture and our democratic institutions and norms, and how profoundly it could unsettle the Jewish condition. I think not just about multiple expressions of the ideology but also about its metastasizing and institutionalization, about how identity politics on the left inflames identity politics on the right and vice versa—a vicious cycle, potentially calamitous, that would compromise liberal democracy and Jewish security, not just in the next election cycle, but also in election cycles for years to come. Today's rapidly expanding normal may seem tolerable to some but, absent a major correction, tomorrow's normal may be much less so.

Losing out to "Equity"

Earlier, I described how the woke concept of equity can implicate Jews in the oppression of other minorities—how, if group disadvantage derives from white supremacy, as anti-racist ideologues claim, so too must group advantage: if categorized as "white," Jews could be accused of oppressing marginalized groups in order to assure their own success in this country and elsewhere. I also explained how equity could be used to significantly reduce the number of Jews in American institutional life and ultimately to disenfranchise American Jewry.

Imagine for a second that you are an American Jewish adult in your early thirties who grew up poor. You lost your father when you were ten years old, and your mother had to work odd jobs to make ends meet. Being Jewish was not easy where you lived; you were subject to taunts and bullying. And you were dyslexic, so you had a hard time learning to read and did poorly in school until your last two years in high school, when you finally figured out, with the help of a caring teacher, how to work around your disability. After high school, you attended the nearby community college, got straight A's, then transferred on a partial scholarship to a state university, where you mopped the cafeteria floors to pay for your basic expenses. You did well in undergrad and went on to get your MBA. After graduate school you got a good job at a major consulting firm. You felt good, having a measure of economic security for the first time in your life. You worked diligently at the firm, received glowing reviews from your supervisors, and were promoted twice. You got married and had a baby.

Sickened by the murder of George Floyd, you attended a local protest with colleagues from the firm. Your company quickly established an "internal equity review" that met in secret for three months, after which the CEO announced that the company would make significant changes in its business practices and in its staff structure so that "we can fully live up to our values of equity and inclusion." You were involved in several important projects at the firm, so you didn't really worry about how these company changes, whatever they might be, would impact you. A few days after word went out, however, your supervisor called you in and without explanation, laid you off. In disbelief, you asked him, "Is this so the company can hire more people from marginalized communities?" He merely stared at you, silent. You had your answer.

This story is mostly true, based on a friend's experience. Taken to its logical conclusion, the woke ideologue's approach to equity will routinely have this kind of impact on people on the losing end. Woke ideology is no prescription for positive race relations or genuine social progress, and its impact on the Jewish community can only be dire.

In a January 2022 interview with Yehudah Kurtzer of the Hartman Institute of North America, *New York Times* columnist Bret Stephens warned that the new equity paradigm could have a devastating impact on the American Jewish community over time. Historically, Stephens argued, because this country was founded by Calvinists who regarded success as a sign of divine providence, thriving American Jews have been granted some measure of respect: "Jewish success in America has tended to lead to admiration, and admiration towards ever greater forms of assimilation, to the point that discrimination has more or less ended." But, Stephens stated, when success is redefined as privilege, as woke ideology does, "and privilege is viewed with suspicion, Jews may also be viewed with suspicion." Stephens pointed to the high percentage of Jews in student population of elite colleges such as Yale, where their numbers far exceed their percentage of the population. "You can say, well, that's because young Jewish students worked hard and got good grades and deserve their places in an elite institution like Yale, or...there's something wildly wrong, this is a privilege that gives one small group a completely disproportionate and an unfair grip on the American meritocracy. If you take the latter view, you're on the road to destroying the conditions which allow Jews to do as well as they have here."[125]

I doubt many Jews who support the equity concept have fully grappled with the possibility that this form of racial gerrymandering may severely limit the numbers of Jews in colleges and companies and displace those already there. This fate is all too familiar to many older Jews—and, more recently, Asian Americans—who were subjected to quotas. For example, New York City's Exam Schools, a collection of nine highly selective public schools, are being challenged by activists who regard the high percentage of Asian American students—upward of 50 percent—as evidence of racial discrimination against Black students. The high percentage of Asian Americans in these schools flunks the Kendi equity test, so—in the woke activist view—their selection methods must be radically altered or shut down. The reality, of course, is that such changes to the Exam Schools admissions process specifically discriminate against Asian students, as do attempts to get rid of Gifted and Talented Programs. These so-called equity-based changes are dimming the prospects of hundreds of thousands of Asian young people and, once the full extent of woke reforms set in, will have similar effects on many Jews.[126]

It's one thing to expand the American meritocracy, to make it more inclusive by actively recruiting more minorities—as Project REAP did in the commercial real estate industry—and to invest in minority communities with better education and job training. We should all support such steps to level the playing field. But we must refuse to downgrade the very idea of merit by hiring faculty and staff, or admitting students, based on race alone and excluding others based on notions of "over-representation." The cumulative effect of the Kendi concept of equity will likely undermine American competitiveness, reduce the prospects of a substantial percentage of American Jews, and generate widespread rancor and resentment among Americans. Jewish community institutions that support this version of equity should hit the pause button and think through the implications.

Excluding Jews from Progressive Coalitions

From 2010–2014, while I was at the David Project, I participated in ongoing conversations with Jewish students and Jewish campus professionals about the ideological atmosphere on campus. Early in 2014, one Hillel (center for campus Jewish life) director, a Progressive who tended to downplay antisemitism on campus, began to change her tune: "Jewish students really are being excluded from social justice coalitions," she acknowledged. "They're being treated like oppressors for simply refusing to condemn Israel or declare themselves anti-Zionists. And I really don't know what to do or say about it. I rarely label campus activities antisemitic. I don't call BDS (the "boycott, divestment and sanctions" movement against Israel) antisemitic. But this feels different. This is completely exclusionary."

In October 2020, the Senate of the University of Illinois Student Government put forward a resolution supporting Black Lives Matter, which a broad swath of the campus community supported. Pro-Israel students wanted to get behind the resolution as well, but language was added that called on the university to divest from companies that sell products and services to the Israeli government. Ian Katsnelson, a leading pro-Israel student on campus, called the resolution "anti-Semitism masked in a cloak of social justice."[127] Jewish students who opposed BDS were effectively shut out from the coalition supporting Black Lives Matter. Such acts of exclusion on campus have been happening for years.

The phenomenon of Jews being excluded from Progressive social justice coalitions may have started on campus, but it hasn't been confined to campus. In June 2017, three Jews holding rainbow Jewish Pride flags with the Star of David were asked to leave the Chicago Dyke March, an LGBT event, because their flags "made people feel unsafe." American flags were also not allowed at the event, but flags from other nations were permitted. Two years later, the DC Dyke March, a social justice-focused parade for queer liberation similarly barred all "nationalist symbols," but specifically naming only the Israeli and American flags. Rainbow flags with Jewish stars were banned because organizers said they were symbols of "violent nationalism" reminiscent of the Israeli flag, which could feel threatening to Palestinian marchers. "We choose to prioritize Palestinian lives and justice in Palestine over lazy symbols," organizers wrote. "Palestinian flags are allowed because we believe they represent the hope for freedom for the Palestinian people," and "The symbols of liberation are the whole point of Dyke March. Symbols of governments that cause human rights abuses are not welcome."[128]

In October 2021, the D.C. chapter of the environmentalist Sunrise Movement withdrew from a voting rights rally in Washington due to the participation of three Jewish groups—the Jewish Council on Public Affairs, the National Council of Jewish Women, and the Religious Action Center of Reform Judaism—stating, in the words of the chapter, "Given our commitment to racial justice, self-governance, and indigenous sovereignty, we oppose Zionism and any state that enforces its ideology." Prior to the march, the Sunrise Movement—the national organization with which Sunrise DC is affiliated–hadn't commented on the DC chapter's position, claiming it hadn't had time for review. But when the chapter published its position in black and white, its parent organization objected in no uncertain terms, calling it "unacceptable and antisemitic."[129] In June 2022, a new antisemitic initiative called The Mapping Project came into being. Aligned with the BDS movement in Boston, The Mapping Project named Jewish organizations, volunteer leaders, and professional staff in an interactive map of "Zionist leaders and powerhouse NGOs." The group says its goal is to demonstrate that "institutional support for the colonization of Palestine is structurally tied to policing and systemic white supremacy here where we live, and to US imperialist projects in other countries." Understandably, Boston area Jewish leaders who have been specifically named on the map are worried that they could become targets of further acts of hate and even of violence. According to Jeremy Burton of the Boston JCRC, the map was "amplified and praised on Twitter by the nonprofit activist group Massachusetts Peace Action." In other words, The Mapping Project, a disturbing escalation of antisemitic rhetoric, hate, and intimidation coming from the anti-Israel, extreme left, has already been validated by an important voice on the progressive left. Numerous Democratic elected officials, such as Senator Elizabeth Warren, were quick to condemn it. Undoubtedly, The Mapping Project does not currently represent the dominant approach of the mainstream left.[130] Perhaps such efforts and incidents are one offs, or perhaps, as the ideology morphs and spreads, they're harbingers for things to come.

"Corbynizing" American Politics

Before 2015, when Jeremy Corbyn came to power in the British Labour Party, most Jews in the UK supported Labour, much as most Jews in the US support the Democratic Party. Corbyn, however, was a known anti-Israel flamethrower, and his election sent shockwaves through the UK Jewish community. In 2009, he referred to Hamas and Hezbollah as "our friends" and, two years later, accused the "Zionist lobby" of pushing for the deportation of Sheikh Raed Salah, the vicious antisemite who claimed that the Israeli Mossad committed the September 11th attacks. In the same year, Corbyn supported a mural pasted on a wall in East

London showing Jewish bankers with big noses playing monopoly on the backs of naked workers.[131]

Once elected, Corbyn's signal to his adherents that they could express Jew-hatred with impunity prompted a significant rise in antisemitic incidents. Many of the 300,000-strong British Jewish community felt deeply insecure during Corbyn's tenure. "We are seeing British Jews increasingly talking about leaving and also seeing signs of people actually leaving, not just to Israel, but also to the United States and Canada—and Australia is a destination as well," said Gideon Falter, chairman of the Campaign Against Antisemitism (CAA). In 2020, in the wake of Labour's resounding defeat in the general elections, the UK-based Equality and Human Rights Commission (EHRC) pointed to "a culture within the party which, at best, did not do enough to prevent anti-Semitism and, at worst, could be seen to accept it."

While it may not be imminent, there's reason to fear a similar fate for the Democratic Party in the US. The November 2018 Congressional elections brought us The Squad, three of the four—Reps. Ilhan Omar (D-Minn.), Alexandria Ocasio-Cortez (D-N.Y.) and Rashida Tlaib (D-Mich.)—all known detractors of Israel. Two of the three have made explicit antisemitic comments. While they are by no means the first Jew-unfriendly members of Congress, 2018 was the first time several were elected in the same cycle, raising concern that there might be a sea change in the works that could fundamentally shift the Democratic Party's stance on Israel. In the Spring of 2019, then Democratic minority whip Steny Hoyer stated to the American Israel Public Affairs' (AIPAC) policy conference that "there are 62 freshman Democrats—you hear me?" he said. "Sixty-two, not three," suggesting that the American Jewish community shouldn't exaggerate the influence of the three radical, anti-Israel members, who cannot shift the party's position on Jewish and Israel-related issues on their own.[132]

Although the Democratic Party has thus far not completely acceded to anti-Israel voices on its left flank (still a small minority of the Democratic members of the House), politics is downstream from culture, and American culture is changing rapidly. Asked about the prospects for the full "Corbynization" of the Democratic Party, political analyst and *National Journal* columnist Joshua Kraushaar stated "[T]here's a clear dynamic of far-left candidates finding success in deep-blue urban districts, guaranteeing a higher baseline of Squad members going forward. That said, that brand of politics is so toxic in many competitive districts that it's unlikely to get a significantly broader foothold. Furthermore, Democrats have a larger 'moderate' constituency within their party that is much more practical (look at Eric Adams, for instance, in New York City) and are less likely to be overwhelmed by extreme candidates in the same way Republicans have been."[133]

It's quite possible that Kraushaar is right, and the erosion of support on the left will be limited to deep blue districts. If the ideological shift on the left continues unabated, however, we can't be sure that moderate wing of the party will stay moderate in response to the growing influence of the woke wing of the party, or that moderates won't desert the party altogether, leaving the radicals to have their way with whoever is left. The octogenarian leadership of the Democrats in Congress can hold the line only so long against a growing left-wing ideological tide. American Jews, particularly Democrats, have a vital interest in countering woke ideology so that the American Jewish community can avoid the fate of the British Jewish community. While British antisemite Jeremy Corbyn may have left the scene of the British Labour Party, his future counterpart in a more ideologically charged US would likely have more staying power.

Empowering a New Diversity Establishment

In May 2021, Jazmin Pichardo, the University of Maryland's assistant director for diversity training and education, put up a series of anti-Israel posts on her personal social media pages claiming that Israel was engaged in an "ongoing genocide and ethnic cleansing of Palestine." Pichardo had recently been put in charge of the University's antisemitism task force. Two Jewish alumni who are members of the university's Jewish Identity Programming Advisory Committee confronted Pichardo about her remarks after she assumed staffing duties over the University's antisemitism task force, which counters anti-Jewish bias on campus[134]. Her command of the antisemitism task force reminds me of comments I've heard by Jews from the former Soviet Union, who speak of how the hostile Soviet state defined for them what it was to be Jewish. Oleg

Ivanov, a Soviet Jewish emigre in his thirties who works for Israel's consulate here in the US, told the JILV in a March 2021 forum that the current ideological environment reminds him in some respects of the Soviet Union. In certain spaces in the US, "Jews are not the ones who are able to define what Judaism is, what antisemitism is. In fact it's antisemites hiding under the thin veneer of anti-Zionism who are defining these things for us."[135]

Universities in the US have increased their DEI staffs dramatically: they average forty-five such professionals at each school. This trend of hiring massive numbers of DEI professionals is not likely to bode well for Jews or for Israel. In a December 2021 Heritage Foundation report, "Inclusion Delusion: The Antisemitism of Diversity, Equity, and Inclusion Staff at Universities," authors Jay P. Greene and James D. Paul argue that the extent to which DEI staff at universities express anti-Israel attitudes is so out of proportion to the topics they tweet about as to constitute antisemitism. To measure antisemitism among university DEI staff, the authors searched the Twitter feeds of 741 DEI personnel at sixty-five universities to find their public communications regarding Israel. For comparison purposes, they looked at the same set's tweets about China.

The report found that "Those DEI staff tweeted, retweeted, or liked almost three times as many tweets about Israel as tweets about China." Of the tweets about Israel, 4 percent were favorable while 62 percent of the tweets about China were favorable. More tweets referenced "Apartheid" in Israel than expressed anything favorable. Human rights violations in China were barely mentioned. Greene and Paul assert that "Frequently accusing Israel of engaging in genocide, apartheid, settler colonialism, ethnic cleansing, and other extreme crimes while rarely leveling similar criticisms toward China indicates an irrational hatred that is particularly directed toward Jews and not merely a concern for human rights." The report concludes that "university DEI staff are better understood as political activists with a narrow and often radical political agenda rather than promoters of welcoming and inclusive environments."[136]

After I posted the study on social media, I was asked if all the tweets critical of Israel came from the same few DEI staffers. I spoke to Jay Greene, who indicated that the tweets, while somewhat concentrated, came from a high percentage of Twitter accounts. In other words, the Israel-bashing was not an isolated, localized phenomenon. The authors do not claim that their study proves beyond a reasonable doubt that the massive increase in DEI staff promotes antisemitism. Rather, they suggest, it's indicative of attitudes many of us have already observed. We would do well to take note of this impending peril for Jews in institutions whose growing DEI departments are dominated by anti-Israel, antisemitic voices.

Corrupting American Foreign Policy

Woke ideology plays out in in American foreign policy in ways that are directly at odds with Jewish interests. In a report called "The Red Green Alliance is Coming to America," the Reut Group (first cited in Chapter 10) describes how woke ideology has been exploited by radical Islamists forces who use it to influence American foreign policy in the Middle East. The "red-green alliance"—the coalescence of Islamist forces and political progressives that originally took shape in Europe, with an anti-Western, anti-American, and anti-Zionist agenda—has now firmly planted itself in this country. Reut points out that in the US this cooperation is accelerated by a process of "progressivization" of Muslim Brotherhood organizations, which are steadily adopting the rhetoric of Progressive politics. Parroting that rhetoric allows them to brand themselves as a Progressive force and to make common cause with woke activists.

The red-green alliance has increasingly adopted a coherent perception of American foreign policy that rests on America's commitment to liberal democratic values, and an emerging consensus in the US to restrain American military engagement around the world. The red-green alliance, however, focuses its criticism almost exclusively on the pro-Western axis of countries—ideological enemies of the Muslim Brotherhood axis led by Qatar and Turkey. The Islamist-Progressive alliance also actively undermines US support for the Abraham Accords, the peace treaties signed in 2019 and 2020 between Israel and several Arab countries.[137] So in addition to fueling antisemitism on the left, woke ideology provides fertile ground for Islamist organizations to increase their influence over US foreign policy in the Middle East. How much influence they gain depends on the further spread of the ideology and the extent of the pushback.

***

The full extent of various impacts to Jewish security and wellbeing discussed here are not guaranteed, but neither are they—absent any intervention—far-fetched. Some have already taken effect in small if not full measure. American Jews are faced with a choice, one put on full display in California, which I will discuss in the next chapter: whether the Jewish community should try to maximize its place in woke ideological circles to mitigate antisemitism within the movement, or instead oppose woke ideology altogether, knowing that ultimately it will generate antisemitism.

CHAPTER 12

WE ARE ALL CALIFORNIANS NOW

Back in the USSR

Elina Kaplan is an education activist in San Mateo County, California, and mother of two young adults. She came to the US from the Soviet Union in 1978 at the age of eleven. She's been a Silicon Valley high-tech manager and held senior roles in social service and Jewish agencies. Like many Jews from the Former Soviet Union (FSU), who tend to be highly averse to revolutionary rhetoric of any kind, Kaplan is extremely critical of—and nervous about—the rise of woke ideology. Kaplan and other FSU Jews get their backs up at claims that the democracy they now live in, that has served them so well, is fundamentally oppressive and racist. They have lived experience in an oppressive society, and whatever shortcomings the US has today don't qualify. For these Jews, woke rhetoric is deeply disturbing: it triggers alarm bells that tell them the country they fled *to* is starting to sound a lot like the country they fled *from*. Another Jew from the FSU, comedian and podcaster Konstantin Kisin, after describing the spectacular failure of the Soviet Union, stated "I am—perhaps understandably—a little hypersensitive to the emerging far left ideology in Western politics, especially when it's made to look so appealing by the Western politicians."[138] According to former Soviet Refusenik Natan Sharansky (when we spoke in November 2021), "American Jews saved Jews from the Former Soviet

Union, and now it's the turn of Russian-speaking Jews to save American Jews [from woke ideology]."[139]

When, in the immediate aftermath of the George Floyd killing, Kaplan first caught wind of California's Ethnic Studies Model Curriculum (ESMC) and saw that it was both hostile toward Jews and ideological to its core, she was outraged. "All of a sudden, I was reading the same concepts and language, in English this time, in the guiding principles of the California Ethnic Studies Model Curriculum," she explained. She was especially shocked to find that the ESMC treated the BDS movement against Israel on par with the Black Lives Matter and the #MeToo movements in this country. An ESMC draft's list of 154 influential people of color made no mention of pacifist/moderates Martin Luther King, John Lewis, or Thurgood Marshall, but it did include revolutionaries such as Angela Davis. It deemed capitalism a form of "power and oppression." In listing various kinds of bigotry, such as "classism, homophobia, Islamophobia, and transphobia," the draft ESMC made no mention of antisemitism. Jewish Americans were nowhere to be found in the curriculum.[140] It had been pushed by radical activists for decades and got a boost in the post-George Floyd racial reckoning. "With the George Floyd killing and the new climate overall in the country, suddenly the critical ethnic studies movement started to gather steam," Kaplan told me in May of 2022. She saw, in this movement and the ESMC campaign, an attempted ideological takeover of the California public school system.

As a Jew who has experienced antisemitism, Kaplan feels strongly that all students must be educated to understand and respect others. A registered Democrat and a political moderate, Kaplan wants California's children to learn about their state's diverse array of ethnic and religious communities while they are students in the largest school system in this country. But that's not what the critical ethnic studies does. Rather than giving voice to California's varied ethnic communities, the ESMC indoctrinates K–12 students into what Kaplan considers a "narrow ideological agenda" that "diverts the focus from local ethnic groups' real obstacles and accomplishments and shoehorns a one-sided advocacy message."[141]

In response, in 2020, Kaplan co-founded the Alliance for Constructive Ethnic Studies (ACES), which counters ideological agendas in ethnic studies and similar curricula, and advocates for a constructive approach to the subject, to "inspire mutual respect, fight racism, and celebrate ethnic accomplishments." Eventually, thanks to the efforts of many in the Jewish community, California's ESMC has been modified from its original blatantly antisemitic posture. Although it no longer explicitly trades in anti-Jewish canards or formally demonizes Israel, underlying the ESMC is a woke ideological framework that divides the world into oppressor and oppressed, teaches opinion as fact, and creates a unmistakable permission structure for anti-Israel, anti-Zionist, and antisemitic sentiment in society. In fact, the ESMC is already being exploited by the same antisemitic forces who tried to push through the original versions of the curriculum, so that California's children are ultimately acculturated into despising Israel and derisive of "Jewish power," as you'll see in the following discussion about "Liberated Ethnic Studies."

What happens in California, of course, never stays in California. If you want to see what large swaths of the country might look like in a year or two, for better or worse, always look at what's happening in California today. On the positive side of the ledger, California was one of the first states that legalized same-sex marriage, thereby legitimizing it for the rest of the nation. On the negative, it's among the first states to be drastically impacted by climate change, with raging wildfires making large parts of the state uninhabitable. And California is one of the first states to fully embrace a far left-wing ideological curriculum for its K–12 public school system that just five years ago would have been laughed out of the classroom. Like avocado toast and the Real Housewives of Orange County, it's coming to your state too.

The Rise of Ethnic Studies

The ESMC did not come from nowhere. Little did we know it had been brewing on the campus scene for fifty years in the ideological ferment of California's universities, waiting for the right moment to break into the mainstream. In 1967, student activist Rudi Dutschke dubbed this strategy the "long march through the institutions," which was amplified by neo-Marxist thinkers, such as the highly influential German-American political theorist Herbert Marcuse.[142] Tammi Rossman-Benjamin, a former professor at University of California Santa Cruz, wrote in 2013—in

"Identity Politics, the Pursuit of Social Justice, and the Rise of Campus Antisemitism: A Case Study"—that on November 6, 1968, the Black Student Union and the Third World Liberation Front at San Francisco State College (now SFSU) "initiated a five-month strike—the longest campus strike in U.S. history—which set in motion a chain of events that changed the face of American higher education."[143] The acting college president of SFSC, S. I. Hayakawa, acceded to the demands and created the nation's first departments of Black and ethnic studies. The strikers maintained that such programs would revolutionize the "white racist" institution and help students combat oppression in their communities. Such strikes took place in other universities across the state and then the country, yielding the same results in college after college. Rossman-Benjamin observed, "Hayakawa's capitulation to the students' demands, which involved contravening the college's own policies and procedures for establishing new academic programs, demonstrated the vulnerability of the university to the kinds of pressure that the students and their supporters had applied, including physical violence and shutting down the university." Without question, the creation of Black Studies, in particular, was long overdue. The problem is that these departments, with few exceptions, emphasized racial and ethnic identity and social justice over the pursuit of reason and knowledge, moving the university away from traditional scholarship and toward social activism.

Rossman-Benjamin cited a 1999 study focused on the African American Studies departments at Temple University and Harvard University. Temple's department of African American Studies adopted an Afrocentric approach, which abandoned traditional scholarly methodology in favor of a "liberating" pedagogy that calls for social change. I saw such a program during my time at Ohio State in the late 1980s, when the Black Studies department brought the radical antisemite Stokely Carmichael to speak. The faculty were squarely behind the program and actively radicalized the students. Harvard's department, however, stuck with traditional scholarship; department chair Henry Louis Gates, Jr. considered the activist programs "intellectually bogus," and insisted on an academically rigorous program of study utilizing traditional scholarship. Gates said he sought to move African American Studies "from a feel-good politically based, ethnic cheerleading orientation to a real academic discipline." But the Ivy League school was the exception to the rule, in the early days.

Rossman-Benjamin stated, "the coupling of political passions with an ideology of victimhood, which was an essential component of the original conceptions of both Black and ethnic studies, fomented political hatreds that targeted groups identified as 'oppressors.' Initially it was 'whites' who were targeted by the political animus of the College's programs. In time, it would also be 'the Jews.'" Rossman-Benjamin then went on in her essay to make a paramount argument of *Woke Antisemitism* seven years before "The Great Awokening": "What the case of black and ethnic studies at SFSU and the other examples cited above suggest is that academic programs that promote ethnic identity and the pursuit of social justice as a central part of their core mission may contribute to the creation of campus climates favorable to the political targeting of those who are deemed 'oppressors.' In the case history presented here, Jews have been targeted time and again as 'oppressors' of choice.'" In other words, when the world is neatly divided into good guys and bad guys, debate and authentic scientific inquiry are shut down, and opposition to the established orthodoxy is demonized—antisemitism is likely not far behind.

The Jewish Dilemma

After being confined inside the walls of higher education for decades, the ideologues behind the ethnic studies movement in California seized the moment of the racial reckoning and pushed ethnic studies in K–12 grades. The highly ideological version of ethnic studies that had taken hold in higher education was now trying to insinuate itself into the K–12 system. A revised ESMC was unanimously adopted in March of 2021 by the California Board of Education.[144] Throughout multiple versions and iterations of the curriculum—first, removing the most offensive material about Jews, then inserting some curricular resources about Jews, and finally tamping down outrageous ideological assertions—mainstream Jewish groups were divided over whether to try to amend, or to oppose, the ESMC overall ideological framework and whether to support the final version if it improved the representation of Jews. Some Jewish groups—such as the Jewish Community Relations Council of San Francisco—fought to include Jewish narratives in the model curriculum, yet in so doing bartered their promise to support the final product; others—such as the American Jewish Committee—opposed the curriculum framework altogether. Groups that opposed the curriculum came under heavy pressure by the Jewish establishment and lawmakers to support the curriculum. In March 2021, the American Jewish Committee (AJC) stuck to its guns and expressed its disappointment with the adoption of the ESMC, calling the fourth and final version of the curriculum "fundamentally flawed." AJC stated, "[R]evisions of curriculum were a salve but ultimately not curative of the fundamental flaws at the heart of the original curriculum, much of which represented a rigid ideological (but sharply contested) world view."[145]

Indeed, the final—supposedly more moderate—version of the curriculum approved by the State Board of Education specifies Guiding Values and Principles that urge students to "critique empire building," "challenge...imperialist/colonialist beliefs," and connect to "transformative resistance," thereby shifting the focus from domestic (US) ethnic studies to a preoccupation with foreign policy and colonialism—thus, dramatically opposed to the objective of the California legislative mandate to build "an appreciation for the contributions [to the US] of multiple cultures." The ESMC includes assigned reading describing civil rights leaders such as Martin Luther King and John Lewis as "passive" and "docile." While most of the blatantly anti-Israel material has been removed, the ESMC still requires students to read Edward Said's *Orientalism* (1978), where Said erases 3000 years of Jewish history by repeatedly equating Zionism with colonialism. But the ESMC offers no critique of Said's position; rather, it includes an article by Jack Shaheen that states "the state of Israel Was Founded on Palestinian Land," with no counterpoint to his argument either.[146]

Once, I would have sided with those trying to amend the curriculum, such as the JCRC of San Francisco, on the promise of accepting the final version, but now I join its opponents. Some Jewish leaders—I should know, I was one—aren't necessarily true believers in woke ideology, but still want to position the Jewish community firmly inside the Progressive tent in order to influence Progressive discourse on Jews and Israel. They point to the fact that Jews, too, are and have been oppressed—not just in this country but also wherever Jews have gone, for thousands of years—and thus should receive membership in the intersectional club. But these efforts to position Jews more favorably have mostly fallen flat. Woke ideology itself, with its implicit omission of Jews as an oppressed group, has become so pernicious and so widespread that mainstream Jewish leaders have little chance to move the needle on Progressive attitudes to Jews and Israel.

This more conciliatory approach to the ESMC among some organizations is the product of a well-developed reflex among mainstream Jewish advocates who often accept "a half loaf" on all manner of issues in the legislative process where no one gets everything they want. Jewish organizations may ask the government for two million dollars in new security funding but receive only one. It's easy to apply the same "half loaf" logic with the ESMC, without a full accounting of what Jewish organizations are acceding to in the process: an ideology that harms society and Jews. Moreover, Jewish organizations in California, particularly in the San Francisco Bay Area, operate in an ultra-Progressive milieu. The networks of relationships they have built over many years, and successfully maintain, are primarily with other Progressive organizations, and are designed to maximize Jewish positioning in left-wing circles and coalitions. As Progressive groups embraced radical woke ideology, Jewish groups that wanted to maintain their standing had to pay lip service, at least, to woke dogma or, in effect, be cancelled by a philosophy that leads inevitably to more antisemitism and undermines liberal principles. So Jewish groups are damned if they do and damned if they don't: they'll lose their influence among Progressives if they don't back the ideology, but will validate an ideology that foments hostility toward Jews—again, even unintentionally—if they do support it.

In the long run, however, Jews will be far more damned if they support the dogma. As woke ideology has become more radical and widespread, the price of admission into Progressive circles has become far too steep: to go along with woke ideology is to countenance its inevitable antisemitic outgrowths and anti-Americanism. Until society rejects the underlying ideology, the Jewish community will play an endless game of whack-a-mole against antisemitic curricula, programs, and incidents, as they pop up everywhere. Thus, the Jewish groups that pushed for changes to the ESMC portrayal of Jews and supported the final, tweaked curriculum, ended up conceding to and normalizing an intensely ideological framework—borne in critical race ideology—that acknowledges and names only oppressed and their oppressors, undercuts critical thinking and debate, and inflames antisemitism.

I don't see the ESMC's revised position on the way Jews are depicted in the curriculum as a victory worth celebrating; rather, I see it as a dangerous precedent. California's ESMC march to woke perdition demonstrates that there's no ducking the excruciating dichotomy of publicly either supporting or opposing official expressions of woke ideology. In fear of cancellation and loss of position earned through years of dedicated work, too many have chosen the former.

Here Comes "Liberated" Ethnic Studies

In October 2021, Governor Gavin Newsom signed Assembly Bill 101, making California the first state to require all its public high school students to complete one semester of an ethnic studies course. Concerned that the legislation provided a way in for radical activists to push antisemitic versions of the ethnic studies curriculum, Jewish leaders managed to convince legislators to erect "guardrails" in order to prevent such an abominable outcome. These guardrails included a provision stating that the legislative intent is specifically that school districts do not use rejected versions of the ESMC (i.e., those versions that berate Jews and Israel).

A joint statement signed by the Jewish community relations councils based in San Francisco and Silicon Valley (along with San Francisco–based Jewish Family and Children's Services and the JFCS Holocaust Center) hailed measures "that will help ensure fair and inclusive courses in our classrooms and prevent marginalization of our and other communities."[147] Just a few months later, however, the radical groups pushing anti-Israel teachings were busy signing contracts with individual California school districts, ready to teach students that Israel is a "settler colonial state." So much for guardrails.

With the ESMC's ideological underpinnings in place, the same people and groups who had authored and promoted those earlier versions of the ESMC—versions so explicitly antisemitic they were unable to pass—were pushing a Liberated Ethnic Studies Model Curriculum (LESMC) that contains even more extreme material than the original. The goal, the drafters explain on the LESMC website, is for teachers "to be part of a larger movement." The LESMC advocates for the approval—by individual school districts—of instructional materials and strategies that glorify revolution and violence, divide *students themselves* into victims and oppressors, dismiss historic and contemporary nonviolent leaders, and promote antisemitism. It refers to "the current apartheid in Israel" and explains that Zionism calls for the "creation and expansion of Israel as a Jewish state" in "historic Palestine," using "any means necessary." The LESMC calls on teachers to "make clear the connections between the struggle for Palestinian rights and the struggles of Indigenous, Black, and brown communities." The LESMC website promotes a curriculum toolkit that refers to "The Anti-Defamation League (ADL), the Jewish Community Resource [sic] Council (JCRC), and Simon Wiesenthal's Museum of Tolerance" as "Zionist organizations" whose "primary goal is to stunt the development of authentic anti-racist curriculum."[148]

In a webinar in the winter of 2022, the LESMC outlined plans to persuade dozens of school districts across the country to adopt its curriculum. The curriculum authors, who defined Zionism as "a nationalist, colonial ideology," claim that there is "current apartheid in Israel" and that Israel's "settler colonialism" has "pedagogical importance," and therefore must be included in an ethnic studies curriculum. The LESMC explains to teachers that "Zionist organizations" try to "silence discussion of Palestine/Israel" and wants teachers to "integrate Palestine" into their curriculum by tracing connections between "Native American history," "gentrification and forced relocation, criminalization of youth," and "hip-hop as resistance," to "settler colonialism in Palestine." I am shocked, but no longer surprised, by the prospect of any California school district permitting its children to be taught antisemitic falsehoods about Jewish organizations, Zionism, and the history of Israel.

LESMC promoters have pressed State lawmakers to enact legislation that would require credentialing of ethnic studies teachers based on an LESMC framework. They've also lobbied the University of California system to impose admission requirements of a curriculum that includes many components from the LESMC ethnic studies high school courses. While the proposed UC admission curriculum requirements do not explicitly name Israel, they draw on ideologically charged language that centers "an understanding of Indigeneity" and "honor[s] anti-colonial and liberatory movements"—language that readily lends itself to defamation of Israel. Currently stalled in the UC Academic Senate, this proposal would effectively force California high school students who want to attend UC campuses to have studied under such a framework in high school. In response to stalling of the effort, the leaders of the Liberated Ethnic studies issued a statement: "We were informed today that the UC will instead be taking a 'broader approach to include diversity, equity, inclusion and social justice courses.' This cannot stand."

Similar ethnic studies curricula with a decided ideological bent are being introduced in state legislatures across the country. Some local Jewish groups will embrace these bills with open arms, hoping to influence the content and ensure that they don't turn antisemitic. Before doing so, however, these groups should take note: dogma always begets ever more extreme dogma. Radical curricula that don't disparage Jews eventually give way to those that do. And woke dogma has spread, as dogmas do. As I have explained, my children's school district—Montgomery County, Maryland, in the Washington, DC, area, home to one of the country's largest Jewish communities—is conducting a new "anti-racist audit" that claims to "strengthen students' sense of racial, ethnic, and tribal identities, help students understand and resist systems of oppression, and empower students to see themselves as change agents."[149] A curriculum that "helps students understand and resist systems of oppression" will inevitably be used to depict Jews and Israel as perpetuating systems of oppression. With a single ideological template as their only tool, students naturally will view Jews in Israel as "settler colonialists." And this variant of antisemitism will spread all the more if children are indoctrinated with the oppressor vs. oppressed ideology from kindergarten through high school.

Mainstream Jews who align yourselves with woke ideologues, it's time to face the reality: they're just not that into you. And even on those rare occasions when the stars do line up just so, and a mainstream Jew influences someone's thinking on the far left or otherwise improves the representation of Jews, we pay a dear price for supporting an ideology that will continue to fuel Jew-hatred for generations to come. It just ain't worth it.

CHAPTER 13

THE ASSAULT ON JEWISH PRIDE

Internalizing Whiteness

Whenever I have to fill out a form that asks me to designate my race and ethnicity, I always experience a momentary identity crisis. I am less than 50 percent European—23andMe has me at 50.4 percent Western Asian—but the Asian designation doesn't feel right either. The limited options of a government questionnaire can't sum me up, yet woke ideology insists that I check the proverbial "White" box because, it claims, my olive skin entitles me to the benefits of a white supremacist society.

Woke ideology insists that Jews not only benefit from white domination but also are complicit in it. It demands that we declare ourselves white because the power structure—the ideology tells us—thinks of us that way: we took advantage of the privileges and opportunity whiteness afforded us, so now we must acknowledge and disavow those attendant privileges. By accepting the notion that Jews are white, we not only downplay antisemitism ("white people cannot really be victims"), we allow others to define us and impose upon us a pseudo-consciousness, and we denigrate and erase the unique qualities endowed by our heritage and the Jewish condition through the ages. It should be obvious that this self-conception of Jewish whiteness. promoted by some in our own community, is no way to imbue fealty to Judaism and the Jewish people in the next generation.

Several months ago, Brandy Shufutinsky, a Black Jewish woman, and I met with the headmaster of a Jewish day school both of our children, now young adults, attended years before. Brandy and I admire the school for the excellent education our kids received there, and we wanted to express our dismay about the school's new anti-racist education plan. We were alarmed to find that the school's DEI curriculum undermines critical thinking, inculcates kids in an ideology that inflames antisemitism, and imparts the canard that Jews are "complicit in whiteness." Brandy's two older sons, now twenty-two and twenty-eight, have grown into passionate Jewish leaders: one in Israel, a veteran of the IDF, the other on his way to join his brother and live and work in Israel. Their mother shocked the headmaster and me both when she calmly observed: "If my sons had studied under the DEI curriculum you're teaching now, they would never have ended up proud Jewish activists." Those boys grew into strong, committed Jews because the school filled them with pride in their Jewishness and strong critical thinking skills. But the school's new DEI curriculum is bound to have the opposite effect on its current and future students.

Moreover, in the "Jews are White" paradigm, American Jews are no longer permitted to take pride in the prominent role the Jewish community played in the Civil Rights era and at other key moments in American history. Some woke ideologues indict Jews who speak fondly of their ancestral contributions to Civil Rights for exemplifying the "white savior complex." Woke ideology insists Jews feel shame for benefiting from an unjust system that oppresses the powerless—i.e., other minorities. When an external force like woke ideology denigrates the Jewish role in society, it's erasure; when Jewish institutions do it, as many are, it's self-erasure. It doesn't take a major feat of imagination to see how this ideological trend will run roughshod over Jewish identity and pride in the future. Few young Jews are likely to feel compelled to sustain a moral tradition mired in the moral taint of whiteness.

Teaching Jews to Despise Israel

Earlier, I discussed how the woke oppressor/oppressed binary acculturates Americans, particularly young people, into anti-Israel attitudes.

Young Jews, of course, are not immune to such influences. A May 2022 poll conducted by the American Jewish Committee found that 23 percent of Jewish millennials reported that the anti-Israel climate on their campuses had forced them to hide their Jewish identity, 46 percent said it had not, and 11 percent claimed there was no anti-Israel climate in the US. Additionally, 28 percent said the anti-Israel climate on campus and elsewhere made them rethink their own commitment to Israel, while 54 percent say it did not.[150]

The simplistic oppression narrative has already badly battered the connection many younger Jews feel toward the Jewish state. Imagine installing that same ideological software not just in colleges, as it is now, but in K–12 education, as proponents of the current DEI pedagogy demand. It will no longer be enough to worry just about how Israel is being portrayed in schools. The school won't even need to mention Israel for the students to see the country through the binary lens—they will have been conditioned to see everything that way. Unless we put a stop to this damaging pedagogy in schools, it will inevitably take a grim toll on how young American Jews perceive Israel. Jewish schools and institutions must, at the very least, steer clear of this Manichean worldview—or, at most, consider it as one of many ways to look at the world.

Dissing the Argumentative Jew

Woke ideology aims to end debate on social issues, particularly the argument over why different groups…differ. In the woke world view, systemic oppression is the only acceptable explanation for group differences. I simply cannot fathom why so many progressive Jews are drawn to a political sensibility that is so flagrantly at odds with the large slice of Jewish culture that questions and debates ideas, the one in which many of them surely were raised. Judaism's entire religious tradition is structured around *Makloket*: arguments about ethical living. The Jew has always questioned the unquestionable and challenged the conventional. It's hard to imagine this country today without the inspirited, vexing, adversative Jew shaking things up by observing and arguing. What the antisemite hates most about us—the refusal to conform—has been our most vital function in society. Our disputatiousness is among the Jews' most powerful expression of our sense of purpose, always to insist on discussion, never letting a point rest until we are satisfied that it has been tried and evaluated from every angle. Now, tragically, many Progressive Jews are the ones demanding acquiescence to a new status quo that brooks no opposition.

In "The Eclipse of Jewish Cultural Power," Touro University professor Thane Rosenbaum addresses woke ideology's specific impact of the creative Jewish persona: "It isn't that Jews no longer occupy important positions in American culture, to say nothing of other fields. What's disappearing from the cultural scene is the Jewish sensibility: its essential broad-mindedness, impish irreverence, openness to difference, and its skill in the art of disagreement.... Today, culture-makers fear being charged with plundering the stories of others, instead of being inspired to tell them. The new woke ground rules are 'Stay in your lane. Do not fictionalize the experiences of people who are not you. Do not write (or speak) dialogue in their voices. Stop imagining the lives of others.'"[151]

Elsewhere in *Sapir*, Bret Stephens reached back to 1919, to American economist Thorstein Veblen's "The Intellectual Pre-eminence of Jews in Modern Europe": For "the intellectually gifted Jew the skepticism that goes to make him an effectual factor in the increase and diffusion of knowledge among men involves a loss of that peace of mind that is the birthright of the safe and sane quietist. He becomes a disturber of the intellectual peace, but only at the cost of becoming an intellectual wayfaring man, a wanderer in the intellectual no-man's-land, seeking another place of rest, farther along the road, somewhere over the horizon."[152] So when woke ideology silences the gadfly, it doesn't only assault liberal values, it is an affront to an important dimension of Jewish identity: our essential character as a people who argue with each other and even, sometimes, with God, as the Biblical name of the Jewish people, "yisra-el," literally means.

Invalidating Immigrant Jewish Narratives

In centering politically progressive narratives, some Jewish groups devalue the narratives of Jews who have come to this country from totalitarian systems such as the Former Soviet Union, the Middle East, Iran, and Latin America. Woke ideology enforced in Jewish settings denigrates the lived experience of these once-oppressed populations. The Reform Jewish movement's trainings in "white affinity" spaces, and the ADL's "Disrupting Bias" programs, would strike many immigrant Jews as bizarre and politically extreme. Ironically, woke ideologues in the Jewish community offer the most traumatized Jews the least amount of succor.

Earlier, I explained that Jews from the FSU, who constitute more than 10 percent of the American Jewish population, are often put off and frightened by woke ideology because it mimics the totalitarian platitudes of their countries of origin. In "The American Soviet Mentality," Soviet emigree and Wilson Center scholar, Izabella Tabarovsky, likened the current mob mentality in the US to what she grew up with in the Soviet Union. "This cultural moment in these United States feels incredibly precarious. The practice of collective condemnation feels like an assertion of a culture that ultimately tramples on the individual and creates an oppressive society," she stated.[153] The Russian-American author and scholar at Boston College, Maxim Shrayer, told me, "We are not living in a totalitarian state and the fact that we aren't could be proved simply by the fact that we're having this conversation. We wouldn't be having this conversation in Soviet Union." Nevertheless, Shrayer is deeply distressed by "the breathing and living space that is being shrunk from both the right and the left.... [I]magine having fought for the right to express yourself fully as a Jew in the Soviet Union, having made a decision that affected our lives and the lives of our children not to go to Israel but to go to the United States—one should not underestimate the difficulty of that decision for some former Refuseniks and really having felt for the past thirty or forty years that America gave Soviet Jews a great deal of not just of opportunities but also breathing room of freedom." Shrayer senses that freedom is at risk in the current ideological environment; as a result, he and his family plan to move to Israel.[154]

Jews of the 75,000-strong Persian Jewish community, who were constantly under suspicion and in peril in Iran for supporting Israel, are no less likely to oppose woke ideology than Jews from the FSU. Same with the 200,000 Latin American Jews living in the US, who are much more likely to assail uncannily familiar woke buzzwords than to uphold the mantle of "Latinx" in a supposedly oppressive American society.

Emphasizing woke ideology is a turn-off to these communities. In bending over backwards to be "inclusive" of Progressives, Jewish organizations are becoming exclusive—and callous—to immigrant Jews. Alienated from mainstream Jewish life, some of these Jews will form their own communities. Others will simply stay away.

Repelling Jewish Conservatives

Karol Markowicz, a columnist and political conservative from the FSU, wrote movingly in *Paloma Media* in March 2022 about being "Adrift from Jewish Spaces": "Our sons attended a Jewish school attached to a very left-leaning synagogue.... [W]e shrugged off their politics.... Sure, the rabbi was a leftist activist, but how much did that really affect our lives? The teachers were the warmest, kindest people and our sons were getting so much out of it. Then in 2018, Jews started getting assaulted daily on the streets of Brooklyn.... Our activist rabbi did not say one word.... You could not pin the attacks in New York City on Trump supporters, so they [Progressive Jews] simply did not care." Frustrated and disappointed, Markowicz left the school and congregation, eventually moving to Florida.[155]

Jewish political conservatives who attend non-Orthodox congregations, and are involved in mainstream Jewish organizational life, have long had to shrug off their politics, at least publicly. But woke hyper-politicization of Jewish life has made such compromises for many increasingly difficult, if not impossible. Jewish spaces can feel like hostile environments for Jews on the center-right, as woke ideology not only politicizes Jewish organizations, but adds a layer of judgment and moral rebuke if they don't play nice. There is no reason, however, that Jewish institutions that operate outside the political realm really need to be so political.

In "How to Curb the Culture War," Yuval Levin, a scholar at the American Enterprise Institute, observed that "displays of partisan allegiance and factional solidarity may have their place, but they do not belong in every place. And out of their place, they can displace other essential goods, and can divide us along lines that render common action and ultimately common life impossible." Levin observes that nearly everyone struggles to engage others, who are on the opposite side of the culture wars, in the spheres of our lives that aren't normally embroiled in cultural conflict: "We find it difficult to conceive of such separate spheres at all," Levin points out. "Everywhere you look, people seem to be dragging culture-war differences into spaces where they don't belong, and in ways that make it awfully hard for us to trust each other, to live together, and to do our common work."[156]

In a strangely controversial opinion piece, "Why I Keep Politics Off the Pulpit," prominent L.A.-based Rabbi, David Wolpe laments, "[A] ll we hear all day long is politics. Can we not come to shul for something different, something deeper? I want to know what my rabbi thinks of Jacob and Rachel, not of Pence and Pelosi."[157] Rabbi Shai Held responded, "Demanding that politics be kept out of shul is like demanding that Torah be kept out of shul."[158] And therein lies the problem: some Progressive rabbis—religiously liberal but ideologically orthodox—seem to believe that their political views have been handed down to them directly from Mt. Sinai with the authority of the divine word. As Jewish life—particularly the liberal movements (Reform, Conservative, Reconstructionist)—has become increasingly ideological, the 25 percent of the Jewish community who vote Republican will become increasingly alienated and grow in numbers. I generally vote with the 75 percent but feel alienated as well.

Shutting Down Discussion of Jewish Continuity

Jews have always debated ways of surviving both the external threat of antisemitism and the internal threat of assimilation. One of the penultimate portions of the Passover Haggadah is the 2000-year-old parable of the "Four Sons" (or "Four Children"): the wise, the wicked, the simple, and the one who does not know how to ask. The parable reflects a contemplative discussion among rabbis, conducted over many generations, about the best way to perpetuate the tradition among Jews of varied levels of commitment and knowledge. And in the wake of the Holocaust, when one third of all Jewish people were annihilated, questions of Jewish survival and continuity are more paramount than ever.

Of course, we have legitimate differences of opinion among ourselves about how best to strengthen and perpetuate the Jewish people. But now even the idea of Jewish survival and continuity is under attack: a woke wing of the Jewish studies professoriate and community activists want to shut down the whole Jewish continuity enterprise that, they insist, was born in patriarchal sin. In the Journal of American Jewish History, Lila Corwin Berman, Kate Rosenblatt, and Ronit Y. Stahl argued that "a Jewish continuity paradigm…treated women and their bodies as data points in service of a particular vision of Jewish communal survival," and that "American Jewish continuity discourse was embedded within patriarchal and misogynistic structures." The authors asserted that "telling women who they can and should marry and when and how often they should have children is what we mean by the patriarchal and misogynistic foundations of the continuity paradigm and its apparatus."[159]

The supposedly ominous "apparatus" that the authors indict is not, however, a totalitarian government forcing people to adhere to some state dogma, or a coercive clergy in a ghettoized community forcing people into submission; rather, it is a set of communal and educational programs such as Birthright Israel, which takes young Jews to Israel in hopes that they'll fall in love with the Jewish state and each other. The doyens of Brandeis and the American Jewish Committee never enacted forced fertility programs or put into effect mandated match-making services. In fact, the "continuity experts" that Berman, Rosenblatt, and Stahl rail against have never enjoyed unparalleled hegemony; multiple points of view have always been entertained at Jewish conferences and meetings and expressed in research by a vast range of scholars representing varied perspectives.

Further in their critique of the continuity paradigm, Berman, Rosenblatt, and Stahl stated, "Instead of interpreting the midcentury indicators of increased Jewish exogamy as a sign of Jews' successful integration…Jewish communal leaders and social researchers responded with rising alarm, worried that these patterns foretold an enfeebled Jewish future." The Jewish scholars and philanthropists who supported such continuity programs, however, fully understood that Jews had successfully integrated. They worried that American Jews had become so well integrated that they would assimilate out of existence. Steven Bayme, the then Director of Contemporary Jewish Life at the American Jewish Committee, explained that "the narrative of assimilation coexists with one of Jews who are very committed and very involved Jewishly.... I would just not take one story without the other."[160]

I wonder whether these scholars who argued for Jewish continuity programs are right to be alarmed that integration brings about "an enfeebled Jewish future"; or whether such integration might strengthen the Jewish community and expand its ranks; or whether the Jewish community should use scarce resources to invest in the "core" of Jewish life, or the "periphery," or all levels equally? One would think these are important questions about which reasonable people might disagree. Yet when even a liberal Jewish writer, Jane Eisner (then editor of *The Forward*) in "Family is a Jewish Value. Don't Let the Mistakes of a Few Rob Us of That Gift," took exception to their view that Jewish continuity is a function of patriarchy, the authors would not argue on the merits. Eisner stated, "If you view child rearing as a burden only women bear, if you view these trends [of diminishing rates of fertility and marriage] as the only natural reaction to women's empowerment—well, I can understand why talk of a Jewish future focused on marriage and family could be seen as patriarchal and confining."[161] In response, Berman, Rosenblatt, and Stahl dismissed Eisner as the naïve dupe of a misogynistic system, claiming that "systems of oppression, we know, can conscript willing and unwitting participants."[162]

Unfortunately, others in the Jewish world are beginning to vilify the Jewish continuity paradigm as well. Tema Smith—then a staff member of 18doors, an organization that empowers interfaith families and individuals—tweeted in December 2021, "We've come so far in acknowledging that racism, homophobia, ableism, classism, transphobia, anti-intermarriage sentiment, etc., have kept people from coming through the doors of our institutions." Here Smith treats "anti-intermarriage sentiment"—presumably efforts to promote in-marriage within the Jewish community—as a category of bigotry on par with racism and homophobia. Under such a conception, anyone who believes endogamy is important to Jewish survival in America can be accused of a new kind of bigotry: "anti-intermarriage sentiment" rooted in a misogynistic social order. These scholars and activists are making it harder for Jewish organizations to identify the policies and strategies that strengthen Jewish life—a prime example of how woke ideology makes it impossible to address real world problems and harms the very people it's supposedly designed to help—in this case, Jews. If this trend keeps up, we won't be able to speak openly about how best to build a Jewish future. A ban on all talk of Jewish continuity could be the next ideological straitjacket for Jewish organizations, subverting Jewishness and undermining Jewish pride.

So woke ideology not only fuels an external threat, it cultivates an internal one as well. Antisemitism's mirror image is internalized Jewish prejudice: Jewish self-hatred. The former Israeli politician and writer Einat Wilf called this phenomenon—whereby society, or a specific segment of society, cajoles Jews into giving up some key aspect of their identities in order to be part of "the Community of the Good"—paying "a pound of flesh."[163] In 20th century America, Jews paid "a pound of flesh" by giving up, at least publicly, their ethnic identity in favor of a purely religious self-understanding. In his seminal 1955 essay, "Protestant, Catholic, Jew," Will Herberg explained: "It was largely in and through... religion that [the immigrant], or rather his children and grandchildren, found an identifiable place in American life."[164] The American pluralism of the early 20th century treated ethnic identity as incompatible with the American project, but endorsed religion as an acceptable outlet. Many Jews obliged by no longer viewing themselves in ethnic or national but in religious terms.

As in the Soviet Union, where Marxist totalitarian ideology required Jews to give up both their religion and ethnic identities to stay in the good graces of the Party, today's Progressive left extracts its "pound of flesh" by demanding that Jews self-identify as white, then mouth pieties against white supremacy, confess to their complicity in it, and surrender their critical faculties and their cultural character, in order not to be canceled, or trolled, or to suffer other indignities that befall dissenters from woke ideology. Some progressive circles ask Jews to abandon their Zionism and support for Israel. In *Jewish Pride: Rebuilding a People*, Ben M. Freeman explained, "This is what antisemitism does to us. It fills us with shame and it forces us to choose between being a member of the wider community or being Jewish—just as Jews today are made to choose between being proudly Jewish or members of the progressive community."[165]

Unchecked over time, woke ideology will impoverish Jewish life by draining it of its most compelling qualities. We may not know the full implications of this for years. I'm not suggesting every woke Jew will become a raging self-hater. Obviously, there are deeply committed Progressive Jews—rabbis and Jewish educators among them. Rather, I'm arguing that, left to its own devices, woke ideology is likely to sap Jewish pride and commitment by demanding that Jews think and behave in ways at odds with authentic and longstanding Jewish sensibilities. Ben M. Freeman put it like this: "The question ultimately is: how can we feel pride in our internal identities when society impulses an external identity upon us that does not relate to the truth of who we are?" We don't have to go along. As Pamela Paresky put it, along with her explanation of conditional whiteness, "We are not required to play the parts that others have written."[166]

***

As with the perils of growing illiberalism in the broader society, the danger of the assault on Jewish pride is not just about what's happening today; it's also about the degree to which woke ideology is allowed to become institutionalized in the future. Have most rabbis, Jewish educators, scholars, professionals, and philanthropists already thrown in the towel or bought into the ideology? Are they on the whole beyond the point of no return? I hope not. I suspect not. We have ample evidence that large numbers of mainstream Jews quietly oppose the stifling discourse. The only way to turn the tide is to identify and rally the silent majority of Jews who still want to be in conversation with each other, and stand up to antisemitism on both sides of the political spectrum.

PART II

SUPPORTING LIBERAL VALUES, COUNTERING ANTISEMITISM

CHAPTER 14

RESTORING JEWISH LIBERALISM

End Spirals of Silence

Early in May 2022, in New York City, I met with a group of a half dozen Jewish women who had traveled sixty blocks south of their homes on the Upper West Side to join me for coffee in Chelsea, the trendy, artsy, LGBT bastion just below Midtown. "I would have been happy to meet you uptown," I told them, "much closer to my hotel."

"Actually," explained Susan, organizer of the meeting, "a couple of us are worried about being overheard or seen with you."

A little surprised, I replied, "I doubt anyone would know who I am." But these women didn't want to chance it, were sufficiently afraid of being seen with me to travel way outside of their normal range. Such is my life these days: many agree with me and support my stance against woke ideology, but few will risk saying so.

In this instance, these women—parents of teens and tweens—were beside themselves, appalled at what their children were being exposed to and learning in their Jewish day schools, specifically the gender identity uproar that their daughters were engulfed in, which these parents believed teachers and school administrators were reinforcing.

"More than 50 percent of the girls in my daughter's eighth grade class identify as gender nonbinary or trans," one of the women told me. "Can you imagine that? The headmaster and the teachers act like it's no big deal and actually support this trend. They won't even acknowledge the controversy around it." I knew exactly what she meant. One of my children went through an excruciating period of gender dysphoria that appeared to come out of nowhere. We would have supported our child's choices in the long run but were concerned that the dysphoria might be a temporary condition and that the system—the school, the therapist, their friends, other parents, Instagram—was pushing them more quickly than they were ready. Everyone around us seemed singularly dedicated to making sure that this child in obvious psychological distress got exactly what he wanted, when he wanted it: puberty blockers, hormones, unadulterated validation that the young teen is exactly the gender he says he is. In a matter of six months, the phase passed. He wasn't trans after all. So I understood exactly why—in a Progressive enclave like upper Manhattan, amid a gender ideology craze—these women would be worried about being spotted with me, when even questioning a rapid shift in gender identity gets one written up as a transphobe.

In 1974, the political scholar Elisabeth Noelle-Neumann pointed out that most of us fear social isolation more than just about anything else that might befall us. Human beings continually observe others in order to suss out which of our opinions will meet with approval or will result in rejection by our social milieu. And some of us exert isolation pressure on others, Noelle-Neumann posited, by rebuking or ignoring them. Against a background of self-silencing intimidation, a vocal minority with strong opinions can be perceived as dominant—perceived, that is, as a majority—if they express their positions adamantly and repeatedly. Others with divergent opinions tend to keep mum when their opinions would expose them to isolation pressure. People who sense that they have public support tend to express their opinions more forcefully and openly. Loudly expressed opinions on one side and silence on the other set in motion what Noelle-Neumann termed the "spiral of silence."[167] When a big push from one direction meets no resistance from the other direction, the spiral expands quickly. And the entire process tends to work subconsciously—that is, those who are silent and those doing the silencing are rarely aware of their roles in the system in bullying or being bullied.

The more I promote liberal values of open discourse in the Jewish community, the more I realize that most people agree with me but don't want to risk subjecting themselves to isolation pressure, so they will find any excuse they can to avoid taking the plunge into authenticity. Sometimes they tell me, "I wish you would focus on X," or "I wish you would say Y differently," or "Too bad so many conservatives support this issue"—but they can't quite pinpoint where they disagree or exactly what makes them squirm, just that they are somehow uncomfortable.

In the Fall of 2021, I reached out to a Jewish professional I have known well for many years and regard as an energetic and creative force in Jewish life. She seemed reluctant to speak when I reached out by email but agreed to a meeting over Zoom. When we finally connected, she told me, "I take pains to make sure that everything I say is stated in the least inflammatory way possible"—an implied criticism of my looser, swing-for-the-fences rhetorical style.

"Why do you feel you have to do that?" I asked her. "Isn't that precisely what I am criticizing in our social discourse?" She thought for a minute, then went on a rant against the censoriousness of the current moment, of her workplace, of her colleagues, of the Jewish community, of society in general. I got the feeling that maybe she wasn't as concerned about being tainted by my critique of woke ideology as she was about admitting that she agreed with me—a heretic—which might make her one too.

Around the same time, a rabbi I knew growing up told me, "Sometimes, David, it seems that your support for liberal values is really a shield for expressing specific views about race and racism." I paused. "Everyone loves viewpoint diversity," I said. "It's diverse points of view that they despise." "Touche!" he chuckled. Other people I talk with are eager to tell me they agree with my diagnosis of the perils of woke ideology and rising illiberalism, but they explain that their work or social situations don't allow for intellectual honesty.

Our central task, then, is to bring these believers in open discourse out of the proverbial closet. In my experience, it can be done, not with everyone but with many, perhaps enough to shift the culture in institutions. In May 2022, when I interviewed Jonathan Rauch—a senior scholar at Brookings, a pioneer in the same-sex marriage movement, and an intellectual force behind liberalism—he explained why JILV and the larger nascent movement for restoring liberal values should take a page out of the playbook of the highly successful LGBT movement:

> Breaking down the closet was the most necessary, difficult, personal, and ultimately transformative element of the gay rights revolution. There were millions of us—"we are everywhere," we always said—but the mere allegation of homosexuality was enough to get us canceled. We'd lose our friends, our reputations, our jobs. The closet kept us isolated, fearful, silent. The first activists to come out had to be brave, but then change happened fast, beginning with the growing confidence they felt and then radiating outward. It turned out not only that were we everywhere but that we could win support everywhere. The rest is history. When I look at the defense of liberal values today, I often see a similar dynamic. Many Americans are dismayed by the intolerance and bullying they see on the cultural left and the authoritarianism and cultism they see on the MAGA right. But they often worry, with reason, that coming out will get them targeted for cancellation, political extinction, even threats of violence. The thing is, though, that the bullies are never as strong as they seem. Too often, we liberals allow ourselves the false luxury of hoping others will stand up to them. That's why moderates are so under-represented and, often, so under-confident. What was true for lesbian and gay people two generations ago is true of the much larger number of liberal pluralists today: being outspoken and unashamed changes the world, and faster than you may think.[168]

While I am still learning what works and what doesn't work in coaxing more people out of the closet and restoring liberal values in Jewish and organizational life, I do have some key observations that, when brought to scale, we can use to shift the discourse. Here are some strategic principles for restoring liberalism to American society in general and to Jewish life in particular.

1. **Connect the dots for others**

   Many American Jews who understand that antisemitism exists on the left have not yet made the connection between woke ideology and the growth of antisemitic sentiment on the left. The problem is that if they don't see the connection, then they'll often look the other way when woke ideology is promulgated in the Jewish organization or congregation. When I posted an article I wrote about the connection between the ideology and antisemitism on Facebook, a friend of many years who worked in the Jewish community messaged me, "That really hits home. It feels much more threatening when it creates antisemitism." In fact, I've learned from dozens of conversations that the "woke ideology fuels antisemitism" idea gets far more interest, attention, and commitment, among most Jews than a critique of cancel culture or institutional dysfunction. Our task, then, is to help Jews and the larger Jewish community draw this conceptual linkage for themselves.

2. **Find Safety in Numbers**

   Only when a critical mass of resistance materializes will woke ideology be exposed as representing the views of a small percentage of the population, and only then will institutions rethink their ideological commitments. To create the safety-in-numbers effect, we need to organize key constituencies—rabbis, Jewish professionals, philanthropists, academics, lawyers, doctors, Jewish LGBT activists, Jews from the FSU, etc.—to push back. The letter signed by 250 rabbis, warning of the dangers of illiberal ideology in Jewish life and the need for conversation, was precisely the type of effort that communicates to others that they are not alone; they have the support of their colleagues behind them. The next step is to organize and encourage those rabbis to move their congregations to embrace viewpoint diversity.

3. Educate the Community

I have found that many people intuitively oppose woke coercion, but lack the information and vocabulary to express their opposition and may not even be fully aware of the entire liberal intellectual tradition that supports their views. We need to expose them to a range of thinkers and ideas that help them put their thoughts into words. JILV, for example, is developing an adult Jewish curriculum called "Makhloket," which brings to light the writing of woke ideologues (Ibram X. Kendi et al.), and of their critics (John McWhorter et al.), so that participants can compare and contrast the opposing arguments and ideas. At JILV, we also impart to participants the rich array of Jewish thought about free expression of ideas and argumentation. We hope that over time a critical mass of educated, more balanced people in Jewish settings will bring about a larger cultural shift. Other such educational endeavors are needed in making a difference.

4. Raise the Stakes

While not a problem specific to the Jewish community, many companies, governments, and nonprofits have instituted Diversity, Equity, and Inclusion (DEI) programs, in no small part to reduce their legal liability in discrimination lawsuits. Unfortunately, most DEI initiatives are based on an illiberal "anti-racist" perspective, which often separates people by race and forces people to accept their complicity in a racist system and acknowledge their privilege. We who are concerned about the spread of woke ideology should fund and initiate lawsuits against DEI initiatives that engage in coercive or discriminatory conduct, such as the cases of Nicole Levitt and Ron Albucher (whom you read about in Chapter 10: both were placed in white affinity groups at their workplaces and told that antisemitism didn't belong in the diversity conversation). Indeed, many current DEI programs are in direct violation of the 1964 Civil Rights Act by practicing discrimination based on race, when they require employees to participate in such affinity groups and declare themselves privileged. Victims in many workplaces will come forward if they know they aren't going to go bankrupt over legal fees. With a robust legal effort in place, we can, over time, shift the balance of risks for individuals facing institutions and incentivize organizations to revise their diversity efforts with more balanced approaches. Forcing companies and organizations to rethink how they do diversity will reduce woke coercion in all institutions, including Jewish ones.

5. Tell Stories

In January 2022, a writer under the alias "N.S. Lyons" wrote a powerful, widely shared blog about how to counter woke ideology:

> In practical politics, narratives are superior to arguments. For example, one could argue that "critical race theory is a neo-Marxist ideology that divides the world into oppressor and oppressed." Certainly, this would engage some readers. But imagine another approach: "In Cupertino, California, teachers forced 8-year-olds to deconstruct their racial and sexual identities, then rank themselves according to a hierarchy of oppression." This formulation connects emotionally, which is the essential precondition for action.[169]

Enforced woke ideology affects individual people on the deepest personal levels. Show it in action, as "Lyons" does here. Make woke theory tangible in its practices, and reasonable people will respond reasonably.

6. Operate as a Network

The recently launched Institute for Liberal Values (ILV) is a consortium of organizations representing different constituencies devoted to fighting for liberalism and against the imposition of woke ideology. National organizations like the Foundation Against Intolerance and Racism (FAIR) and the Foundation for Individual Rights in Education (FIRE) play an important role in opposing ideological bullying, and organizations representing specific ethnic or racial groups—such as Free Black Thought—challenge the claim that all minorities are ideologically and politically homogeneous. Collaboration among groups is increasingly crucial in strengthening the liberal project in America and keeping dangerous ideologies in check. We need to continue to build not just individual organizations, but also a robust network that cooperates around a set of best practices and common strategies. As my friends at the Reut Group are fond of saying, "It will take a network to defeat a network."

7. Conduct Focused Advocacy Campaigns

Some institutions that have embraced woke ideology are more susceptible to change than others. A large foundation backed by a woke philanthropist is not likely to change directions from a pressure campaign any time soon, because the foundation has little if any political or financial exposure. Its only constituency is the donor or donors behind it. A mainstream Jewish organization or school with a diverse set of stakeholders, however, is much more likely to bend, mainly out of concern that it not alienate specific constituencies or individuals. We should start with the low-hanging fruit. Begin by talking to the powerful members of the organization. Be forthright and diplomatic. Find like-minded people within the organization and ask for their help. Only go public if all else fails. Don't take your foot off the pedal.

8. Advance Alternative Modes of Diversity

Opposing wrongheaded woke-inspired "diversity" is not enough; we must build alternative models that incorporate viewpoint diversity alongside representational diversity. We must advance an inclusive vision of society that encourages open discourse, addresses legacies of racism and bigotry, and reduces disparities over time. Such a vision will highlight what unites us rather than what divides us. If we can succeed in moving our institutions away from coercive models, the truly inclusive model should be waiting in the wings.

Individual Action

Each of these strategies described will require a robust network of activists and philanthropists. Our community's and country's liberal values are on the line. Every one of us must ask ourselves what we can personally do. Here are several examples:

1. **Do no harm**

    Michael Powell of the *New York Times*—on the *Persuasion* podcast with Yascha Mounk in November 2021—spoke of his coverage of the illiberal ideological environment at Smith College. In an article for the *Times* months earlier, Powell had interviewed several faculty members at Smith who privately opposed the school's growing illiberalism. Powell said after his article came out, that the college president denounced Powell's piece at a faculty meeting. One of the faculty members Powell interviewed for his *Times* piece called him a few hours after the meeting, amused, and "named a number of people who stood up and denounced the piece and several of those were people who had given me chapter and verse on the problems at the university."[170] I've seen people offer such phony approval for woke platitudes in Jewish organizational settings as well. If you cannot bring yourself to oppose the ideology publicly, at the very least don't publicly pretend to support it.

2. **Close Your Wallet and Open Your Mouth**

    At a JILV meeting in May of 2022, a parent whose child experienced problems in her school's coercive DEI program told the other parents present, "Close your wallet and open your mouth." Stop your financial support, in other words, and tell the institution exactly why you are no longer giving them money, at least until they change the way they operate. Donors and parents are much more powerful than they realize, especially if they band together. Just as it took only a few woke ideologues to impose their views on the institution, it may take only a few upset parents to reverse course. I tell people to be more public than you're comfortable with. As with any challenging endeavor, people who take risks over time develop thicker skin. In the winter of 2022, a Jewish professional agreed to come on a Zoom meeting with other Jewish professionals to discuss the current illiberal atmosphere in their field only if he didn't have to appear on the video or use his real name. Seeing his colleagues speak openly gave him the confidence to do both: he decided to turn on the video and use his real name. In future meetings, he was quite outspoken.

3. **Do the Awkward Dance**

In order to find like-minded people you can work with, you have to do the awkward dance: asking questions or making subtle (or not so subtle!) hints that express your displeasure with the imposition of woke ideology. I have done the dance more times than I can count, as when I was told of a DEI professional at a university, a Black woman with rather unorthodox approaches to diversity. I reached out and set up a Zoom conversation. I didn't know her precise views going into the discussion, so when we spoke, I started my critique of standard DEI practices slowly: "I have concerns that some practices are coercive," etc. "Yes, me too," she stated. As the conversation proceeded, each of us gradually expressed ourselves more openly until we realized that we agreed on nearly everything. Each of us now had a new ally. To find new allies in this struggle, there's no getting around that awkward dance.

4. **Raise Your Hand**

Jewish organizations tend to embrace coercive DEI programs when a combination of staff and board members push them through. Too often, non-woke political liberals and conservatives fail to speak out against these efforts. In mainstream Jewish settings, these non-woke board members are often focused solely on holding the line on the organization's stance on Israel, fearful that the woke Progressive wing will have its way. They trade silent acquiescence on domestic policy for public support on Israel policy. Until recently, these board members didn't view illiberal diversity pronouncements and policies as a threat. Now many realize that the ideology behind these initiatives spawns anti-Israel and antisemitic sentiment, and they are increasingly willing to challenge it. The best way of stopping such bad policy and training programs in your organization is to raise your hand and ask the tough questions: Does this training reflect our values? Why are we undertaking training that tells everyone what they must think about complicated issues? Does this program embrace a simplistic narrative that might lend itself to spreading antisemitism?

Even better, do the awkward dance and find other Board members who agree with you and will back you up at the meeting.

5. **Practice These Five Words**

When people make adamant woke pronouncements in public, they can intimidate others into silence. These five words, "I think about it differently," let you introduce an alternative viewpoint without sounding shrill yourself. Practice makes perfect.

6. **Be Like Elina**

Recall Elina Kaplan, the education activist I told you about, who pushed back against the woke ethnic studies curriculum in California. She created a new organization and mobilized thousands of parents into action. We need more brave, motivated, and strategic activists willing to counter the ideology and strengthen liberal values. Consider being one yourself.

7. **Write an Opinion Piece and Send It In**

Many of you are superb writers. Put those skills to work by churning out 700 words that make the case for liberal values and shed light on woke antisemitism. We need your voice. Start with your local Jewish paper or local newspaper.

8. **Show Up at Challenging Moments**

   Sometimes, everything is on the line—at a school meeting, a vote on a new "racial justice" policy, or discussion over a new DEI initiative. We must seize these opportunities by showing up and speaking up, with our powers of reason and civility. For sure, the ideologues on the other side of the issue will be there, ready to make their points, and if you're not there, they will have the microphone all to themselves.

9. **Build Something New**

   Some institutions and organizations become so shot through with woke ideology that they are past the point of no return. They simply can't be salvaged, at least until the cultural winds blow in the opposite direction. In such cases, consider founding and forming alternative institutions—schools, synagogues, advocacy organizations, etc.—that reflect liberal values. Example: along with a new university being built in Austin, Texas, a new (but unrelated) Jewish day school in the same city will focus on the liberal intellectual tradition and Jewish thought.

Individually and collectively, we can stop the spirals of silence and turn the tide of woke ideology. Now is the time for each of us to join the effort.

CHAPTER 15

RECLAIMING JEWISH SOCIAL JUSTICE

A Little Social Justice

In January 2022, I came across a new book, *The Social Justice Torah Commentary*, an anthology of essays by various rabbis and Jewish social justice activists on issues such as racism, climate change, mass incarceration, immigration, disability, women's rights, and voting rights. The book is meant to be a guide for weekly Torah study and probably is a rich source of material for sermons. I didn't read all the essays, but the ones I did read provided an interesting take on Jewish texts and concepts. I don't agree with every point made in the collection, but I regard such commentary as a completely legitimate way to look at Torah in light of contemporary moral and social realities. (As a criminal justice reform and mental health advocate, I especially appreciate Rabbi Joel Mosbacher's riff on the Torah Portion *Acharei Mot*, where he addresses the overrepresentation of people with severe mental illness in our criminal justice system.)

But then I came across a *Times of Israel* article from December 2021 by Rabbi Barry Block, who edited *The Social Justice Torah Commentary*, and I was reminded of precisely what's wrong with contemporary Jewish social justice discourse and, perhaps, with the book itself. Referencing the battles over the way race and racism are taught in K–12 schools, Rabbi Block said that as a rabbi he is "troubled by this assault on the concept of social justice, which Jewish religious leaders have been championing for longer than the term has existed. The truth is," he explained,

> that social justice is a noble and worthy concept that has every place in our classrooms and our broader society. At this critical time in our nation's history—when many Americans have a renewed understanding of the extent to which systemic racism has infected our nation, while many others willfully close their eyes to that harsh reality—embracing our Jewish tradition of social justice has never been so pressing.[171]

Last I checked, nowhere in the voluminous commentary on social issues in the Jewish tradition is there a single mention of the term "systemic racism." To be sure, racism is a perfectly valid explanation of disparity among different groups in society. But it is not the only explanation. Attributing our social ills to "systemic racism" alone ignores the crucial role played by poverty and socio-economic status (especially generational wealth), family structure in segments of inner city communities, unintended negative effects of well-intentioned government programs, and the sheer amount of time it takes for a community that has experienced centuries of oppression to rise out of its previous conditions. Indeed, insisting that there is a single way to understand group outcomes and that anyone who disagrees or cites alternative explanations is "willfully closing their eyes" is mind-bogglingly illiberal. This is gospel, not commentary.

This woke, shrunken conception of social justice—I call it *Tikkun Olam Hakatan* (a small *tikkun olam*—the Hebrew term for making the world a better place)—excludes from its covenant millions of American Jews who want to better the human condition, but may not agree with this woke formulation about what needs to be fixed or how to fix it. We shouldn't all have to agree on exactly what ails society or on the origins of those social problems in order to be part of the social justice fold. According to the Pew Survey of 2020, 45 percent of politically conservative Jews say that social justice is essential to their Jewishness. Seventy percent of very liberal Jews agree.[172] If social justice weren't so closely linked to a particular ideological and political agenda, imagine how many more conservatives might emphasize it. Nearly half do already.

Shortly before the party primaries in 2015, I met with Jewish social justice activists who were asked what they envision for the future of their movement. One said, "I know we will be on our way when Elizabeth Warren becomes president." Others nodded in agreement. There is nothing wrong, of course, with hoping for a more progressive president. Many do. But such an expression does not exactly lure in non-Progressives. I doubt there are many Jewish social justice circles, where a conservative with alternative views on making the world a better place would feel entirely welcome.

My friend Leon is a Jewish political conservative who is deeply committed to supporting people with disabilities; he volunteers an untold number of hours to the cause and donates thousands of dollars every year. While Leon recognizes that American history is replete with racial discrimination and that such discrimination persists in certain sectors, he doesn't believe—and not for lack of consideration of the evidence—that systemic racism exists in America today. While I do not agree with Leon that there is no systemic racism in society, I know his heart is in the right place and I honor his support of people with disabilities as being in the best tradition of Jewish social justice. And I don't think his "wrongthink" on systemic racism should bar him from some exclusive Jewish social justice club for the ideologically pure. Anyone can feed the hungry and not agree with the systemic racism explanation of disparity. Anyone can welcome the stranger and not agree with that explanation of disparity. Anyone can work to change our criminal justice system without believing that our system is fundamentally racist.

What's missing from *The Social Justice Torah Commentary*—not just from the book but also from the philosophy—is any consideration of the many, many ways people can work for social justice and make the world a better place. The Talmud—the original commentary on Torah—is a collection of thousands of arguments among rabbis, and then even more arguments by later rabbis about what the earlier rabbis were arguing about. One would expect that progressive Jewish thinkers would emulate this mode of commentary and argumentation about how best to lift people up. One would hope that their vision of a more perfect world would include people with whom they disagree, just as the rabbis in the Talmud did in their time.

In "Judaism and the Politics of Tikkun Olam," Rabbi Yitz Greenberg held that

> [T]here is no one "kosher" Jewish approach to social justice, just as there is no single authorized Jewish response to any of the challenges we humans encounter and create for ourselves. Jewish texts contain a multitude of opinions, enough to support the presuppositions and political persuasions that almost any seeker could bring to them. One can write a purely socialist economic plan for society using only traditional Torah sources. One could also write a capitalist model citing another set of Torah sources. I suggest we do neither.... Instead, I propose that we embrace Judaism's multiplicity of perspectives, its real-world wrestling with human complexity and imperfection. As Rabbi Israel Salanter wrote: "To live up to the Torah's ideals, maximally, one must develop every human capacity and insight—and its opposite" (*Ohr Yisrael*, Letter #30).[173]

"Nothing about social justice should be controversial," Rabbi Barry Block tells us in *The Social Justice Torah Commentary*. I disagree; on the contrary, everything about social justice should be controversial. Through controversy and argument, we develop both better insights and more creative solutions to our social ills. In Talmudic times, the rabbis understood this in their own context. Too many in today's progressive rabbinate don't. The problem with modern Jewish social justice discourse is not that it doesn't add anything valuable to Jewish life—it has much to add—but, rather, that it claims an absolute monopoly on the truth and regards anyone who disagrees as "willfully closing their eyes."

Fortunately, we have shining examples of Jewish social justice leaders making space for ideological diversity, like Rabbi David Stern, senior rabbi of the Reform Temple Emanu-El in Dallas—the largest synagogue in the southern US—who has enlisted politically conservative Jews in his social justice community. His community leans more conservative than most, which requires of its leader a measure of political deftness and ideological flexibility. Whenever a contentious issue comes before the Dallas Emanu-El synagogue, such as whether to be a sanctuary congregation for undocumented immigrants, Stern engages conservative members in shaping the congregation's response. During a May 2019 webcast, I asked Stern about broadening the social justice tent. He replied, "As soon as we isolate it (social justice) to a particular political agenda, we are not only making ourselves less effective, but we are not being who we are supposed to be as a community."[174] In other words, Jewish social justice can't live up to its billing without being truly inclusive of multiple viewpoints.

The Missing Conservative Voice

Here's where Jewish conservatives need to do their part. Many political conservatives have ceded the social justice territory by treating the very notion of Jewish social justice with derision. Along with other conservative critics, Jonathan Neumann, author of the controversial *To Heal the World?: How the Jewish Left Corrupts Judaism and Endangers Israel*[175] ignores, even sneers at, the fact that social justice is deeply embedded in the Jewish tradition, alleging that a "tiresome fixation on *tikkun olam*...has allowed Judaism to fall into disrepair." Neumann goes as far as to claim that "the truth is that *tikkun olam* and its leftist politics have no basis in Judaism."[176] In an October 2018 blog post in *eJewish Philanthropy*, Andres Spokoiny, CEO of the Jewish Funders Network, argues persuasively that "[V]irtually all the prophets talk tirelessly about the need to create a just and ethical society; many of their words sound pretty much like a 21st-century *tikkun olam* manifesto."[177] Judaism cares deeply about a just society and always has. Who would want to be part of a spiritual and moral tradition that didn't? Certainly not many young Jews, whom we are trying so hard to attract.

And Jewish conservatives have a crucial role to play. I remember well the late so-called "bleeding-heart conservative" congressman and Housing Secretary Jack Kemp, whose signature idea in the late '80s and early '90s was to establish Urban Enterprise Zones designed to drive businesses into poor areas and provide opportunity for minorities. We need to hear more from conservatives like Kemp, but they seem to have gone into hibernation. To be sure, there are individual researchers and writers who continue to advance ideas and policy prescriptions to close disparities and alleviate poverty. But we don't hear nearly enough from such conservative thinkers who would be immensely valuable in developing market-based solutions to poverty, inequality, health care, and climate change. Whether one buys into these policy ideas or not, conservative innovators like Kemp would enrich our political and communal discourse and refocus our politics on searching for real solutions.

Jews once played an outsized role in conservative politics that reverberated throughout the nation. Jewish neoconservatives of the 1990s and early 2000s infused conservatism with a progressive spirit by embracing a can-do attitude toward democratization and social mobility. Whether you agreed with Paul Wolfowitz (Deputy Secretary of Defense under George W. Bush) and his actions during the war in Iraq, he was motivated to make the world a better place by spreading freedom and democracy in autocratic lands. Jewish neocons were both skeptical of government-supported poverty reduction and insistent we not give up on effective alternative solutions lifting people out of poverty. The late neoconservative thinker Nathan Glazer stated in the 1998 documentary *Arguing the Word*, "I look at policies that are trying to improve welfare; I think you must keep on trying even if you have not had great success."[178] Reading Glazer's body of work, one sees a tenacious Jewish conservative social justice warrior looking in earnest for solutions that will bring some measure of relief to stubborn social problems.

Irving Kristol and Norman Podhoretz, the godfathers of neoconservatism, believed the neoconservative movement had been so successful in influencing mainstream conservative thought, that they could give up the "neo" in neoconservative. Over time, neoconservatism lost its distinct Jewish quality. A conservative Jewish concern for equality and social well-being, however defined, would be a welcome voice in US politics today. A politically conservative Jewish social justice voice would allow for more bipartisanship on issues on which conservatives and liberals might agree.

A Big Tent Social Justice

Every once in a while, we are reminded of the bipartisan spirit that once was. At a criminal justice reform conference in September 2018, Democratic Representative Hakeem Jeffries of New York spoke eloquently about the critical role Republicans played in passing the First Step Act, legislation that shortens sentences for deserving prisoners and provides job training. In December 2018, Republican Senator Chuck Grassley of Iowa observed, "Several decades ago, Congress passed well-intentioned laws imposing harsh mandatory sentences to stop the flow of drugs in our communities. I voted for those laws. But they've [the drug laws] had some unintended consequences."[179] The more conservatives see themselves in the business of repairing the world, the more liberals and conservatives will discover where they intersect and can compromise. A big-tent Jewish social justice approach would allow for deeper, more complex arguments among people who have different views about addressing social problems. That big tent would elevate democratic discourse, not just social equality, which would truly make the world a better place. We'd have better solutions because an assortment of ideas would be publicly vetted. It would be fine—even healthy—if these two versions of Jewish social justice, politically liberal and politically conservative, battled it out in the marketplace of ideas over the best way to lift people out of poverty or to solve the climate crisis. Such a debate ought to be Jewish music to our ears. In conducting Jewish arguments on social issues, we could model arguments for the sake of heaven for the rest of society.

Rabbi Yitz Greenberg has said,

> I want to offer an alternate way for American Jewry to apply the Jewish tradition in the movement to expand social justice in America. Rather than cherry-picking sources to support one "side" of an issue or the other, let us consciously utilize both liberal and conservative elements in the tradition and offer a balance of the particular and the universal, retaining a simultaneous focus on Jewish interests as well as on broader concerns. By

> appreciating that the tradition has much to say on many sides of these issues, I hope to enable both wings of American Jewry to find common language for engaging more constructively and respectfully.... Judaism combines a liberal, utopian, universal vision of completely transforming the planet with a conservative, realistic, particularist method of transformation."[180]

Jewish congregations and organizations who do social justice need not engage in a one-size-fits-all version of social justice. It's time for the non-woke majority of Jews—traditional liberals, moderates and conservatives alike—to reclaim the mantle of Jewish social justice and build upon a common cause with other groups outside the Jewish community who share our worldview and our democratic vision for American society. The country needs our voices.

CHAPTER 16

REBUILDING A JEWISH AND AMERICAN CENTER

The Failure of Progressive Engagement

The rise of the Boycott, Divestment, and Sanctions (BDS) movement against Israel in the early 2000s alarmed mainstream Jews, not so much because BDS could hurt Israel economically as because it could isolate the Jewish state on the left in this country and around the world. To counter this growing threat, American Jewish advocates identified key non-Jewish segments on the political left they deemed "fence-sitters" on Israel, and began to cultivate their support. In an influential 2010 report, the Israeli think tank, the Reut Group, recommended that "Israel and its allies should maintain thousands of personal relationships with political, financial, cultural, media, and security-related elites," and added, "Israel should engage its critics, while isolating the de-legitimizers."[181] Fence-sitters included, among others, segments of African Americans, mainline Protestants, Latinos, and LGBTQ activists. The American Jewish advocates aimed to engage these groups on social justice issues that are as essential to them as they are to many Jews and to persuade them off their fences on the side of Jews and Israel, away from supporting BDS and other extreme anti-Israel positions.

However, when a resurgent and radicalized Black Lives Matter movement began to take shape in 2013, many in the Jewish community, me included, started to worry that the Progressive fence-sitter strategy was faltering. Far from engaging mainstream Jews, the rising extremist rhetoric was highly divisive: they wanted to abolish, not reform the police; to malign, not repair, institutions; to endorse radical anti-Israel voices, not advance Israeli-Palestinian peace. And the challenge wasn't just from the shrillest voices. For moderate Progressives to retain standing on their issues, they had to uphold many of the radicals' ideological demands. The venerated Black civil rights organization, The National Association for the Advancement of Colored People (NAACP), announced it was revitalizing its image to appeal to younger people—the Associated Press reported in January 2020—demonstrating the pull of these ideological trends.[182] As the radical forces have seized center stage and declared themselves the standard bearers of Progressive politics, moderate Progressive constituencies have rapidly distanced themselves from Jewish organizations who refuse to conform to the ideological demands of the moment.

Now, in our post-George Floyd environment, we see that the strategy of engaging Progressive activists has largely failed: in the past five years, Progressive attitudes toward Israel have markedly worsened. Mainstream Progressive groups now embrace many of the dangerous woke concepts I've discussed here: promoting Kendi's version of equity, demonizing whiteness, linking identity to privilege, and centering one narrative above all others to the point where, unfortunately, these woke social justice concepts are now completely baked into Progressive coalition politics. Jewish groups undertaking Progressive engagement should admit to themselves that what may have seemed like it could work for Israel and for Jews in Progressive engagement just a decade ago is not working now. In view of the scourge of antisemitism and anti-Israelism we saw during the Israel-Hamas conflict in Gaza in May 2021, we can't argue that we've made any headway at all in checking left-wing anti-Israel sentiment. As I pointed out earlier, the ascending ideology—its fixation on the oppressor-oppressed binary—inoculates Progressives against traditional lines of argument, messaging, and story-telling from pro-Israel Jews. Woke ideology renders previously amenable segments of non-Jews (and even Jews) unreachable.

Aligning the American Jewish community too closely with the Progressive movement, especially insofar as such alignment requires conformity to its woke pieties and credos, gives succor to an ideology that will ultimately harm us. We saw the cost of conformity earlier in the California

Ethnic Studies controversy that would have delegitimized thousands of years of Jewish history by installing a "Black oppressed versus White oppressor" binary into the impressionable minds of children and then classifying Jews as white. Therefore, supporting or even paying lip service to a radical, woke ideological framework—one that sees America and the West as supremacist—is far too high a price to pay in order to prevent Progressives from excoriating Jews and Israel. And in the long run, it'll fail.

Strengthening the Illiberal Right

What's more, the left's identitarian tendencies—its insistence that marginalized people get to define oppression for the rest of society; its preoccupation with white privilege and equity; its dubbing political opponents "fascists" and "racists"—feeds and will continue to feed right-wing white identitarian tendencies, which can generate horrific violence and fuel radical politics. When Progressives gloat that America's majority population will be non-white in twenty years, thus propelling the minorities into power for eternity (unlikely the case, given the number of Latinos and other immigrant voters moving to the political right), and when woke ideologues crow that people of color will replace whites as the dominant culture, they feed already seething paranoia among insecure whites who fear that they will indeed be "replaced." Replacement Theory or "The Great Replacement"—the right-wing ideology that holds that immigrants and people of color are seizing white entitlements for themselves—is growing in popularity. An AP-NORC poll released in May 2022 reveals that

> [O]ne in three (32%) adults agree that a group of people is trying to replace native-born Americans with immigrants for electoral gains. A similar share (29%) also express concern that an increase in immigration is leading to native-born Americans losing economic, political, and cultural influence."[183]

The gunman in the May 14th mass shooting in Buffalo, New York, Payton Gendron, stated in his 180-page manifesto that he wanted "to spread awareness to my fellow whites about the real problems the West is facing." He continued, "[T]his crisis of mass immigration and sub-replacement fertility is an assault on the European people that, if not combated, will ultimately result in the complete racial and cultural replacement of the European people."[184] Of course, nothing can possibly justify or rationalize Gendron's extremist politics and murderous rage, but we must create a culture that makes such scenarios less likely. Woke ideologues may think they are "punching up" at whites—many of whom have been left behind in the race to the American Dream, who live in communities with rampant drug addiction, minimal education, and few economic prospects—but many members of that segment of the white population of this country just feel punched, never mind from what direction, and some feel they are justified in punching back. Dogma on the left not only begets more extreme dogma on the left, it also begets more extreme dogma on the right.

While American Jews alone cannot stop this vicious cycle, at the very least we can refrain from partaking in it. We can, instead, articulate a unifying narrative—an alternative to both the left's and right's noxious grievance-mongering and one-upmanship. We can—in political scientist Yoscha Mounk's words—promote a "cultural patriotism" or what I call "Patriotic pluralism" that brings people together, celebrates rather than denigrates the ways cultural groups influence each other, upholds democratic principles and ideals, and acknowledges America's flaws and, instead, builds on its manifold strengths.[185]

Bad Partners

Fighting antisemitism has always meant forging alliances and building coalitions, bilateral and multilateral, to face down extremists and to send them scurrying back under their rocks. The nearly 100-year-old Jewish Community Relations Council of Philadelphia (JCRC), for example, describes its work as being grounded in cultivating relationships and seeking partnerships with different faith and ethnic communities throughout Greater Philadelphia. "Through partnerships, events, community programs and discussions," the mission statement reads, "JCRC works with partners from all faith backgrounds on issues of shared concern, including bigotry, anti-Semitism, systemic racism, homophobia, Islamophobia and religious extremism."[186] This statement gives a sense not only of what the JCRC is doing—fighting antisemitism and extremism—but also with whom they are doing it: Progressives.

Except now with the rise of woke ideology, our would-be partners on the left are advancing the very ideology that foments antisemitic sentiment. Even though many Progressives would gladly join the Jewish community in condemning antisemitism coming from the right, they cannot be good allies in fighting Jew-hatred if they're advancing a dogma that promotes antisemitism—however implicit—in their own camp. The same can be said about the "replacement right": while many on the replacement right would enthusiastically condemn antisemitism on the woke left, their own ideology fuels Jew-hatred on the right and thus rules them out as reliable allies. By the same token, joining forces with the woke left doesn't make Jews safer, it makes us less safe, just as joining forces with the replacement right would make us less safe. Jews will be safer when we work with allies who share our interests in shoring up the institutions of democracy, safeguarding the marketplace of ideas, and countering extremist voices on both ends of the political spectrum.

A Rebuild-the-Center Strategy

Steve Windmueller, a longtime thought leader in Jewish community advocacy and relations, observed in September 2021:

> A major Jewish political reset is underway at this time, focusing on domestic affairs, foreign policy considerations and the increasing diversity that defines the Jewish communal orbit. When the political environment is as unsettled as we find today, such new structural initiatives are likely to reframe the conversation, refocus policy options, and grow the diversity of the community. These new institutional voices are seeking to establish a middle ground between the political extremes.[187]

Jewish leaders with longstanding ties to Progressive groups often suffer from a psychological block against imagining different coalition partners. They've come to see Progressive ethnic and religious leaders—a very thin slice of their own populations—as the only representative and authentic spokespeople of the oppressed. Given the growing hostility to Jewish interests on the left, it's time for Jewish organizations to branch out and identify new partners, groups of people who haven't been overwhelmed by ideological fads and can still talk to one another, groups who are predisposed to condemning antisemitism, no matter where it crops up or hides.

Some of these new allies may be Democrats and others Republicans. During the Covid-19 pandemic, some may have supported mask mandates in schools and others may have opposed them. Some may favor sweeping healthcare reform and others more modest market-based solutions. People in this new centrist coalition already have at least one thing in common: they are all committed to democratic norms and liberal values. They vow to protect civil liberties from excesses on both the right and the left. They guard their tongues from extreme and delegitimizing rhetoric: they don't call people they disagree with "racists" or "libtards."

Our new allies may or may not be religious, but they operate on the principle of good faith whenever possible. They are wary of radical proposals that would fundamentally alter democratic institutions and norms. They do not buy into woke dogma on the left or replacement theory on the right, and they are willing to entertain alternative points of view about what ails society. These new allies of ours are more concerned with alleviating social problems than in being ideologically pure. They are patriotic but not bombastically nativist; they understand America's weaknesses as well as its strengths, its failures, and its successes. The allies we seek know the difference between an imperfect democracy and a truly oppressive regime, a distinction that is easily lost at both ends of the ideological spectrum. Notwithstanding their differences of opinion and priority, they are capable of working together on a common agenda and fighting together against a common set of threats.

The chart below represents the necessary paradigm shift the organized Jewish community must make in building a new American center.

Old Work	New Work
Targets the political left	Targets the political center
Focuses on social justice issues/fighting racism	Focuses on preserving democratic values/fighting extremism

Strategy: position Jewish community in progressive circles and win over fence-sitters on Jews/Israel	Strategy: mobilize allies on liberal values and strengthen existing allies of Jews/Israel
Sees itself as naturally allied with the left	Assigns itself the task of rebuilding the center
Works within the left-wing ideological framework to maximize Jewish interests	Understands that the left-wing ideological framework is as inherently problematic as rightwing ideologies, and opposes both

Our new friends may be specific segments of ethnic communities, such as Asian Americans, parents, heterodox Black thinkers, and Latino business leaders. They may be Muslims, Christians, Hindus, atheists, or agnostics.

Who are these new partners? They're people like Indian immigrant Siva Raj and his wife Autumn Lootijen, who organized a recall of three powerful members of the San Francisco school board.[188] On February 15, 2022, nearly 70 percent of the city's voters recalled three school board members. Siva and Autumn's strategy: with a dessert recipe, they launched a "brownie-powered" recall campaign on Facebook that garnered 8,500 supporters. At issue were parents' frustrations with the Board's failure to reopen schools in a timely fashion after the Covid-19 lockdown. The board had spent much of the pandemic focusing on woke-inspired issues such as renaming forty-four schools, including those named after "oppressors" Washington, Jefferson, and Lincoln, and ending the merit-based admissions process at Lowell High School, where Asian students are the majority.

The recall effort also tapped into a wider feeling of discontent in San Francisco, where rising crime and attacks on Asian Americans indicated a dysfunctional and poorly run city. "[The recall] seems to have catalyzed a broader general public awareness in San Francisco," stated Raj. "Many people are seeing what's happening in the school board as a reflection of a broader failure." He continued, "Here we are, living in one of the wealthiest cities in the world, and we are not getting the basics right." Adding to the rancor, one school board member came under fire for anti-Asian comments on Twitter. The tweets, which predated her time in office, stated Asian Americans used "white supremacist" thinking and were racist toward Black students.

Raj and Lootijen are political moderates who stand up for functional schools and push back against woke notions of renaming schools that would erase American history.[189] They, and not the people who were recalled, are the Jewish community's natural allies.

Our new partners are people like Erec Smith, a Professor of Rhetoric at York College and founder of Free Black Thought: a group of scholars, technologists, parents, and an array of American citizens determined to amplify vital Black voices that are rarely heard on mainstream platforms. Years ago, Smith wrote an essay that chronicled his social rejection "for the crime of inauthentic blackness," making the argument "for a radical individualism based on self-regard." In responding to his work, Smith stated, "a prominent rhetoric scholar literally changed my words to make me seem easily refutable and quite pathetic—to prove that blacks attempting to transcend labels suffer from internalized racism."[190]

This conflict arose from Smith's May 2021 essay, "Free Black Thought: A Manifesto," where he stated:

> Black people from all walks of life find themselves deferred to by non-blacks—as if, in one black philosopher's words, "my racial category tied me more 'authentically' to an experience that neither of us had had." But of course, black people are not all the same. Most of them have not been victims of police violence, and most of them don't live in inner cities or in poverty. Thus, black people certainly don't all "feel" or "experience" the same things. Nor do they all "experience" the same event in an identical way. Finally, even when their experiences are similar, they don't all think about or interpret their experiences in the same way.[191]

Smith continued, "The creators of Free Black Thought believe, in the words of Brittany Talissa King, 'there isn't a narrative, one black narrative—there's 40 million.'" He observed that racial essentialism has:

> Gained ground in some schools. For example, in one elite school, students "are pressured to conform their opinions to those broadly associated with their race and gender and to minimize or dismiss individual experiences that don't match those assumptions. These students report feeling that "they must never challenge any of the premises of [the school's] 'antiracist' teachings.... [P]arents are justifiably worried about such innovations. What black parent wants her child to hear that grading or math are "racist" as a substitute for objective assessment and real learning? What black parent wants her child told she shouldn't worry about working hard, thinking objectively, or taking a deep interest in reading and writing because these things are not authentically black?

Erec Smith is a serious thinker and political moderate. He supports reforms to the system and opposes extremism from the left and the right. He's a superb ally of the Jewish community.

These new partners may be outliers in their own communities or, more likely, part of a silent plurality. They are often not the people with the biggest megaphones. These moderate forces may just be getting organized, only recently realizing that they have much to lose by remaining silent. Our new friends will stand by our side whenever antisemitism rears its ugly head, whether it comes from the left or the right, because they too are concerned about the same extremist forces targeting their communities. They too want a stable, peaceful, pluralistic, meritocratic, compassionate, and moderate American society.

Obviously, none of this will be easy. It will require the Jewish community to move out of a comfort zone that is no longer comfortable. It will be like moving to a new city and making a new group of friends, not knowing whether or when we will feel at home again. We can take sustenance from Jewish history, which is full of examples of moving and re-establishing. Our customary place in the Progressive coalition, as it is currently, is not sustainable. Neither are most Jews going to find a home in the populist right, which has its own antisemites, extremists, and conspiracy theorists, some armed and violent. It's time to build a new political home out of a new political network.

This chart depicts the necessary shift in priority partners.

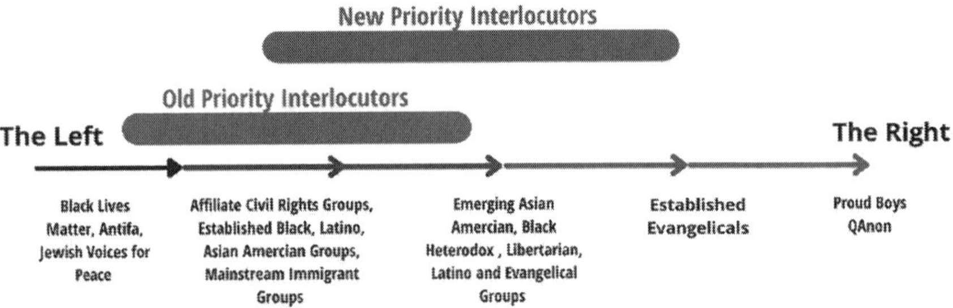

Some will say that the Jewish advocacy arena is already devoted to building the center. Indeed, the idea of "holding the center" is not new, but lately the mainstream Jewish community has focused squarely on engaging the Progressive left. Others will say that these two objectives—reaching out to fence-sitters (are there really many left?) on Israel and building the center—are not mutually exclusive. Perhaps not, but they are in tension, as the price for appeasing radical Progressive demands is high. On balance, however, I still favor some diversification, with different people doing different work.

Rebuilding the center, however, should become the main attraction and not the sideshow of Jewish community relations and advocacy. Our new would-be allies bear a striking resemblance to who we used to be: the Jewish community before it became riddled with ideological factions, petty disagreements, and partisan politics. The old Us, while far from perfect, didn't defer to illiberal ideologies or sacrifice our core principles. We didn't stifle dissent. We debated ideas in the spirit of *Makhloket L'shem Shamayim*: arguments for the sake of heaven. In hitting the strategic reset button and engaging these new partners, we may just rediscover ourselves.

NOTES

1 Helen Pluckrose and James Lindsay, *Cynical Theories: How Activist Scholarship Made Everything about Race, Gender, and Identity—and Why This Harms Everybody*, Pitchstone Publishing, August 25, 2020
2 Ibid.
3 Francis Fukuyama, *The End of History and the Last Man*, Free Press, 1992
4 Ira Glasser on Free Speech, Real Time with Bill Maher (HBO), Jan 28, 2022, https://www.youtube.com/watch?v=x0Lc5b8Flto
5 Free Speech Nation, Interview with Robert Shibley of Fire, June 12, 2022, https://twitter.com/i/status/1536134252399579136
6 Justia, Columbus Bd. of Educ. v. Penick, 443 U.S. 449 (1979), https://supreme.justia.com/cases/federal/us/443/449/
7 Orlando Patterson, "What Have We Learned About Culture, Disadvantage and Black Youth?", Oct 4, 2016, https://www.youtube.com/watch?v=We3hLvOLjl4
8 Andrea Dworkin, *Intercourse*, The Free Press, 1987
9 Shirley Frondorf, *Death of a Jewish American Princess: The True Story of a Victim on Trial*, Villard, June 12, 1988
10 Stokely Carmichael, Jewish Virtual Library, https://www.jewishvirtuallibrary.org/stokely-carmichael
11 Lecture at the Washington Institute for Near East Policy, circa 1994
12 Francis Fukuyama, *The End of History and the Last Man*, Free Press, 1992
13 Charles Krauthammer, "The Unipolar Moment: America and the World 1990," *Foreign Affairs*, Sept. 18, 1990
14 Sidney Goldstein, "Profile of American Jewry: Insights from the 1990 National Jewish Population Survey," *American Jewish Yearbook*, 1992
15 Bruce A Phillips, *Re-examining intermarriage: Trends, textures, and strategies*, January 1, 1997
16 Jean-Paul Sartre, *Anti-Semite and Jew*, Schocken Books, 1944
17 David Bernstein, "Jews on Campus rise to the challenge," Washington Jewish Week, May 2003

[18] Elihai Braun, "UN World Conference against Racism, Racial Discrimination, Xenophobia and Related Intolerance - Durban, South Africa (August 31-September 8, 2001)," Jewish Virtual Library

[19] Jonathan Rosen, "The Uncomfortable question of Anti-Semitism," *New York Times Magazine,* November 4, 2001

[20] Durban Declaration and Programme of Action (2001), UN Human Rights Office of the High Commissioner

[21] Student Nonviolent Coordinating Committee (SNCC): April 15, 1960 to May 1, 1971, Stanford: The Martin Luther King, Jr. Research and Education Institute

[22] Farrakhan: In His Own Words, ADL, January 2013

[23] Million Man March, Brittanica, https://www.britannica.com/event/Million-Man-March

[24] David Bernstein, "Farrakhan: The Torch of Hatred," *Washington Post*, October 21, 2000

[25] Discussion with Mike Bush, April 2022

[26] Children in Crisis: The Failure of Public Education in the District, District of Columbia, Financial Responsibility and Management Assistance Authority, November 12, 1996, https://www.washingtonpost.com/wp-srv/local/longterm/library/dc/control/part2.htm

[27] Yascha Mounk, *The Great Experiment: Why Diverse Democracies Fall Apart and How They Can Endure,* Penguin Press, April 19, 2022

[28] Albert Murray, *The Omni-Americans: Some Alternatives to the Folklore of White Supremacy*, Library of America, February 4, 2020

[29] The Color of Fear (Part 1), Lee Mun Wah

[30] Jena McGregor and Eli Rosenberg, "Trump's crackdown on training about white privilege draws broad opposition Business, nonprofit and civil rights groups have all denounced his executive order," *Washington Post Business*, October 29, 2020

[31] Frank Dobbin and Alexandra Kalev, "Why Diversity Programs Fail," *Harvard Business Review*, July–August 2016

[32] David Bernstein, Memo to AJC Colleagues, "Immigration and American Values," March 3, 2001

[33] David Bernstein, "Consistent Moral Message Missing," *Washington Jewish Week*, January 2003

[34] David Horovitz, "In the rise of a gutsy Arab kid from the Galilee, many harsh truths for Israel," *Times of Israel*, August 24, 2012

[35] History Channel, "This Day in History: August 9, 2014, Michael Brown is killed by a police officer in Ferguson, Missouri," https://www.history.com/this-day-in-history/michael-brown-killed-by-police-ferguson-mo

[36] Quoted in *The Dish*, https://andrewsullivan.substack.com/p/transcript-jonathan-haidt-on-social

37 Kimberle Crenshaw, "Demarginalizing the Intersection of Race and Sex: A Black Feminist Critique of Antidiscrimination Doctrine, Feminist Theory and Antiracist Politics," The University of Chicago Legal Forum 140:139-167, 1989

38 David Bernstein, "The anti-Israel trend you've never heard of," *Jewish Telegraphic Agency*, January 4, 2016

39 Chloe Sobel, "Co-opting social justice won't erase reality in Israel," *New Voices*, , January 20, 2016

40 Grappling with Intersectionality, May 4, 2016, https://www.jewishpublicaffairs.org/conference-call-on-intersectionality/

41 Barry Oshry, *Seeing Systems: Unlocking the Mysteries of Organizational Life*, August 12, 2007, Berrett-Koehler Publishers, August 12, 2007

42 Mari Cohen, "Jewish Groups Embrace BLM, With Conditions," *Jewish Currents*, June 23, 2020

43 I wrote about this episode in "My Cheshbon HaNefesh for Cowardice in the Face of Wokeness," the *Jewish Journal*, March 2021

44 David Bernstein, "Four Reasons to re-engage in the civil rights movement," *Jewish Week*, October 2016

45 Jonathan Haidt and Greg Lukianoff, *The Coddling of the American Mind: How Good Intentions and Bad Ideas Are Setting Up a Generation for Failure*, Penguin Books, August 20, 2019

46 James Gordon, "NY Times does Not fire star COVID reporter who used N-word while leading school trip because it wasn't 'malicious' - just one week after editor was booted for pro-Biden tweet," *Daily Mail*, January 29, 2021

47 Jesse Singal, "More Warning Signs in The Culture Of Journalism: The reaction from Don McNeil's colleagues is just as disturbing as his firing," *Singal-Minded*, February 6, 2021

48 Ira Sheskin and Arnold Dashefsky, "How Many Jews of Color Are There?" *eJewish Philanthropy*, May 17, 2020

49 Rabbi Rick Jacobs and Chris Harrison, "The Reform Jewish Movement Stands with Jews of Color–Period," *eJewish Philanthropy*, May 19, 2020

50 "Jewish Americans in 2020: U.S. Jews are culturally engaged, increasingly diverse, politically polarized and worried about anti-Semitism," Pew Research Center, May 11, 2021

51 David Bernstein, "Do Jewish Organizations Still Need Offices?" *eJewish Philanthro*py, June 2, 2020

52 Quoted in Blocked and Reported podcast, May 7, 2021

53 "A Letter on Justice and Open Debate," *Harper's Magazine*, July 7, 2020

54 Email exchange, July 2020

55 Ryan Grim, "Elephant in the Room," The Intercept, June 13, 2022

56 Michelle Alexander, *The New Jim Crow: Mass Incarceration in the Age of Colorblindness*, The New Press, January 7, 2020

[57] Race and Ethnicity Terms & Definitions, Amherst College, https://www.amherst.edu/campuslife/our-community/multicultural-resource-center/terms-and-definitions

[58] Marc Dollinger, *Black Power, Jewish Politics: Reinventing the Alliance in the 1960s*, Brandeis University Press, June 5, 2018

[59] "Antisemitism in the Classroom: What we can learn from California," Online Event, December 14, 2001

[60] Batya Ungar-Sargon, "A new intelligentsia is pushing back against wokeness," *The Forward*, July 20, 2020

[61] SpeechCast: A Crisis in Moral Authority, Batya Ungar Sargon EP07, Jun 23, 2021, https://www.youtube.com/watch?v=IZHLn_Lizy8

[62] "Jewish organizations say: black lives matter," *Medium*, Aug 28, 2020

[63] Quoted in Khaleda Rahman, "Will Anti-Semitism Undermine the Black Lives Matter Movement?" *Newsweek*, July 24, 2020

[64] Edmund Lee, "Bari Weiss Resigns From New York Times Opinion Post," *New York Times*, July 14, 2020

[65] Bari Weiss, "Stop Being Shocked: American liberalism is in danger from a new ideology—one with dangerous implications for Jews," *Tablet*, October 14, 2020

[66] Bari Weiss, "Meet the Renegades of the Intellectual Dark Web," *New York Times*, May 8, 2018

[67] David Bernstein, "The Dangers of Woke Harm-Based Morality," *Areo,* November 23, 2020

[68] Robin DiAngelo, *White Fragility: Why It's So Hard for White People to Talk About Racism*, Penguin, February 7, 2019

[69] Jonathan Tobin, "Can liberalism be saved from cancel culture?" *Jewish News Service*, March 9, 2021

[70] Matt Taibbi, "Meet the Censored: Kara Dansky," TK News by Matt Taibbi, June 8, 2022

[71] John McWhorter, *Woke Racism: How a New Religion Has Betrayed Black America*, Portfolio, October 26, 2021

[72] Nikki Graff, "Most Americans say colleges should not consider race or ethnicity in admissions," Pew Research Center, February 25, 2019

[73] Eli Yokley, "More Gen Zers Have Negative Views About Capitalism Than of Critical Race Theory

[But] opinions regarding America's latest cultural debate are largely undeveloped among its younger cohort," *Morning Consult*, July 8, 2021

[74] David Bernstein, "Six questions Jewish organizations should contemplate before taking a stand on racial and critical social justice," *eJewish Philanthropy*, March 10, 2021

[75] A Letter to our Fellow Jews on equality and liberal values, May 2021, https://jilv.org/be-heard/

76 Arno Rosenfeld, "Jewish 'Harper's letter' tied to opaque foundation, Republican megadonor," *The Forward*, May 07, 2021

77 Dr. Brandy Shufutinsky and David Bernstein, "An open letter to the Charles E. Smith Jewish Day School," *Washington Jewish Week*, October 13, 2021

78 David Bernstein, "Cancel Culture, Jewish Educators Style: Apparently, DEIJ initiatives in Jewish schools are not open for discussion," *Jewish Journal*, October 22, 2021

79 Monica Osborne, "Will rabbis' statement spark a moment of reckoning for the Jewish community?" *Jewish Journal*, January 16, 2022

80 Gabriel Katz, "Jew vs. Jew: On the real lessons of the Hanukkah story," *Common Sense*, November 28, 2021

81 What Gives Podcast, Felicia Herman: From Jewish History to Jewish Philanthropy, April 26, 2022

82 Matt Bruenig, "Identitarian Deference Continues to Roil Liberalism," *Medium*, Jul 17, 2020

83 Interview with Barry Shrage, April 4, 2022

84 Eli Yokley, "More Gen Zers Have Negative Views About Capitalism Than of Critical Race Theory But opinions regarding America's latest cultural debate are largely undeveloped among its younger cohort," *Morning Consult*, July 8, 2021

85 Interview with Barry Shrage, April 4, 2022

86 Joshua Kraushaar, "Biden's agenda disconnected from voters' everyday reality," *National Journal*, May 27, 2022

87 Joseph Ax, Gabriella Borter and Joseph Tanfani, "A Reuters Special Report: School boards get death threats amid rage over race, gender, mask policies," *Reuters*, Feb. 15, 2022

88 Hannah Natanson, "How and why Loudoun County became the face of the nation's culture wars," *Washington Post*, July 5, 2021

89 JCPA2022 Workshop: The Rise of Local Extremism, Apr 26, 2022, https://www.youtube.com/watch?v=jqfuaMJtF1A

90 "What is Critical Race Theory and Why Is it in the News So Much?" ADL, November 15, 2021

91 "Teachers union pledges to teach critical race theory in all 50 states," Metro Voice, July 6, 2021

92 "How Should I Talk About Race in My Mostly White Classroom?" ADL, September 6, 2017

93 Disrupting Bias in Education, August 12, 2021, https://adl.zoom.us/rec/play/riZEH747q3kb-JbZPTximxNVD-s_ZFYA0UaF0lKoVnrzKriEfqozggMNa2r9SuX62qiMDoKY8cgWyIL4.Rux4qAvoWJeuMSpT

94 From a March 10, 2022 email titled "Clergy Learning Opportunity"

95 Nylah Burton, "White Jews: Stop Calling Yourselves "White-Passing," *The Forward*, July 02, 2018

[96] Dara Horn, "At Harvard, Facts Are For Losers: It turns out that nobody's SAT scores can provide immunity to propaganda," *Common Sense*, May 8, 2022

[97] Andrew Sullivan, "The Anti-Semitism In Anti-Whiteness: Whoopi Goldberg just brought it out into the open," *The Weekly Dish*, February 4, 2022

[98] Deborah E. Lipstadt, *Antisemitism: Here and Now*, Schocken, January 29, 2019

[99] Batya Ungar-Sargon, "When Wokeness Comes for Israel," *Newsweek*, May 13, 2021

[100] Tirhakah Love, "'Jeopardy!' Host Mayim Bialik's Ugly History of Shaming Weinstein's Victims and Being an Anti-Vaxxer," August 12, 2021

[101] EEOC complaint shared with me by the plaintiff, Nicole Levitt

[102] Interview with Nicole Levitt, March 27, 2022

[103] Daphna Kaufman, Eran Shyshon and Adi Levy, "Erasive Antisemitism: A New Threat Arising Within Contemporary Progressive Discourse - Policy Paper – Version A," March 8, 2021

[104] Dr. Pamela Paresky, "Critical Race Theory and the 'Hyper-White' Jew," Sapir, Spring 2021

[105] Jenny Gross and Neil Vigdor, "ABC Suspends Whoopi Goldberg Over Holocaust Comments," *New York Times*, Feb. 1, 2022

[106] "Gazi Kodzo - Anne Frank Hater, Stop Antisemitism," May 16, 2020, https://www.stopantisemitism.org/antisemite-of-the-week-2/antisemite-of-the-week-gazi-kodzo-anne-frank-hater

[107] Twitter exchange, July 9, 2022, https://twitter.com/JHWeissmann/status/1545864006094790658?s=20&t=fqxq_xOU4q7XvvWC9dr2FQ

[108] Hen Mazzig, "How Jewish Twitter users and celebrities took down a virtual anti-Semitic mob," *NBC News*, July 15, 2020

[109] Philip Clark, "Senate Erupts In Anti-Semitism Debate," Stanford Review, April 4, 2016.

[110] Danya Ruttenberg, "Why do white supremacists hate Jews? Because we Jews can fight them," *Washington Post*, August 16, 2017

[111] Dave Schechter, "What is 'Jewish Privilege?' It's complicated," *Atlanta Jewish Times*, August 10, 2020

[112] Ibram X. Kendi, *How to Be an Antiracist, One World*, August 13, 2019

[113] Anna Keating, "The Problem with "Western" Religions on Campus: The strange politics of administrative antiracism," *The Hedgehog Review*, May 4, 2021

[114] Paresky, "Hyper-White' Jew," Sapir, Spring 2021

[115] Beyond All Reason: The Radical Assault on Truth in American Law, Oxford University Press, October 30, 1997

[116] Overview of Complaints Filed Against Stanford University, Louis Brandeis Center for Human Rights Under the Law, June 15, 2021, https://brandeiscenter.com/wp-content/uploads/2021/06/Stanford-Case-Materials-6-15-21.pdf

[117] "Inside the Woke Meltdown at One Domestic Violence Organization," July 22, 2022
[118] Dr. Natalie Hopkinson, "The Women Behind the Million Man March," *New York Times*, Oct. 17, 2020
[119] Natalie Hopkinson, Twitter, https://twitter.com/NatHopkinson/status/1317908612086419457?s=20&t=TqYRisREzeFut7fjdw2mdA
[120] Gabe Friedman, "Jenny Slate leaves Netflix's 'Big Mouth' because her character is biracial Jewish actress calls her role in animated series an 'act of erasure of Black people,'" *Times of Israel*, June 25, 2020
[121] "Equity Through Accuracy: Changes to Our Hate Map," Southern Poverty Law Center, October 08, 2020
[122] "Alt Right: A Primer on the New White Supremacy," ADL, February 10, 2016
[123] Jonathan A. Greenblatt, "Antisemitism on the left is subtler than on the right. But it's getting worse," *Washington Post*, October 27, 2021
[124] Isaac Luria, "Why Addressing Antisemitism Requires Fighting for Justice," *Sources*, Spring 2022
[125] Identity/Crisis Podcast, "Challenging Wokeness: Jews & the American Narrative," Yehuda Kurtzer and Bret Stephens, January 11, 2022
[126] "The NYC Exam School Controversy," Glenn Loury and Wai Wah Chin, The Glenn Show, Oct 22, 2021, https://www.youtube.com/watch?v=PzZ6xJUHAXg
[127] Greta Anderson, "Jewish Students Claim Civil Rights Violations," *Inside Higher Education*, October 26, 2020
[128] Ben Sales, "The controversy over the DC Dyke March, Jewish stars and Israel, explained," *Jerusalem Post*, June 8, 2019
[129] Arno Rosenfeld, "Environmental group boycotts voting rights rally over inclusion of Zionist groups," *The Forward*, October 20, 2021
[130] Andrew Lapin, "Boston Jews say a pro-Palestinian group's map of local Zionist leaders and powerhouse NGOs leads to antisemitism," Jewish Telegraphic Agency, June 8, 2022, https://www.jta.org/2022/06/08/united-states/boston-jews-say-a-pro-palestinian-groups-map-of-local-zionist-leaders-and-powerhouse-ngos-leads-to-antisemitism
[131] Maya Carlin, "Has the American mainstream already been 'Corbynized'?" *JNS*, June 9, 2021
[132] Zack Budryk, "Hoyer says AIPAC remarks were 'misinterpreted,'" *The Hill*, March 25, 2019
[133] Email exchange, May 11, 2022
[134] Alex Nester, "University of Maryland's Anti-Semitism Task Force Chief Has History of Anti-Semitic Statements
Diversity officer said Israel was engaged in 'ongoing genocide and ethnic cleansing of Palestine'," *The Washington Free Beacon*, February 26, 2022
[135] Jewish Voices from the Former Soviet Union (FSU): Why we value the free expression of ideas, May 24, 2021, https://jilv.org/fsuevent/

[136] Jay Greene, Ph.D. and James Paul, "Inclusion Delusion: The Antisemitism of Diversity, Equity, and Inclusion Staff at Universities," Heritage Foundation, December 8, 2021

[137] "The Red Green Alliance is Coming to America," The Reut Group, January 10, 2022

[138] Konstantin Kisin, *An Immigrant's Love Letter to the West,* Constable, July 14, 2022

[139] Interview with Natan Sharansky, November 24, 2021

[140] Jeremy Beaman, "Soviet immigrant says critical race theory uses 'the same concepts and language' as Marxism by Energy and Environment Reporter," *Washington Examiner*, July 31, 2021

[141] Interview with Elina Kaplan, May 11, 2022

[142] Mike Gonzalez, "The Long March Through the Corporations," Heritage Foundation, March 26th, 2021

[143] Tammi Rossman-Benjamin, "Identity Politics, the Pursuit of Social Justice, and the Rise of Campus Antisemitism: A Case Study," Manuscript Version of Chapter 18, *Resurgent Antisemitism: A Global Perspective*, Edited by Alvin H. Rosenfeld, Indiana University Press, June 19, 2013

[144] Ethnic Studies Model Curriculum, California Department of Education, https://www.cde.ca.gov/ci/cr/cf/esmc.asp

[145] American Jewish Committee (AJC) Statement on California State Board of Education Adoption of Ethnic Studies Model Curriculum, March 18, 2021

[146] Analysis from the Alliance for Constructive Ethnic Studies, provided May 2021

[147] Jewish Community Statement on Assembly Bill 101, October 8, 2021, https://jcrc.org/uploads/pr10_8_2021.pdf

[148] Analysis from the Alliance for Constructive Ethnic Studies, provided May 2021

[149] Antiracist Audit to Examine and Address institutional Racism in Montgomery County Public Schools (MCPS), February 2, 2022, https://www.montgomeryschoolsmd.org/departments/publicinfo/community/school-year-2021-2022/Community-Update-20220202-antiracistaudit.html

[150] Zvika Klein, "1/4 American Jewish millennials distance themselves from Israel to fit in," *Jerusalem Post*, April 25, 2022

[151] Thane Rosenbaum, "The Eclipse of Jewish Cultural Power," *Sapir*, Summer 2021

[152] Bret Stephens, "Is There a Future for American Jews?" *Sapir,* Autumn 2021

[153] Izabella Tabarovsky, "The American Soviet Mentality: Collective demonization invades our culture?" *Tablet,* June 15, 2020

[154] Interview with Maxim Shrayer, October 2021

[155] Karol Markowicz, "Adrift from Jewish Spaces," *Paloma Media*, March 5, 2022

[156] Yuval Levin, "How to Curb the Culture War," *Comment*, April 7, 2022

[157] Rabbi David Wolpe, "Why I Keep Politics Off the Pulpit," *Jewish Journal*, June 2017

[158] Rabbi Sharon Braus, "What you call Politics we call Torah," *Jewish Journal,* July 2017
[159] Lila Corwin Berman, Kate Rosenblatt, Ronit Y. Stahl, "Continuity Crisis: The History and Sexual Politics of an American Jewish Communal Project," *American Jewish History,* Johns Hopkins University Press, Volume 104, Numbers 2-3, April-July 2020
[160] "Study finds American Judaism in decline," The Associated Press. September 26, 2003
[161] Jane Eisner, "Family Is A Jewish Value. Don't Let The Mistakes Of A Few Rob Us Of That Gift," *The Forward,* September 17, 2018
[162] Berman, Rosenblatt, Stahl, "Continuity Crisis," 2020
[163] Einat Wilf, "The BDS Pound of Flesh: Using lies and social pressure to force students to disavow Israel is a strategy aimed at raising the psychic and professional cost of being Jewish," *Tablet,* May 10, 2022
[164] Will Herberg, "Protestant--Catholic--Jew: An Essay in American Religious Sociology," 1955
[165] Ben M. Freeman, *Jewish Pride: Rebuilding a People,* No Pasaran Media, February 15, 2021
[166] Paresky, "'Hyper-White' Jew," Sapir, Spring 2021
[167] "The "Spiral of Silence" Theory," https://noelle-neumann.de/scientific-work/spiral-of-silence/
[168] Interview with Jonathan Rauch, May 20, 2022
[169] N.S. Lyons, "No, the Revolution Isn't Over: None of the fundamental drivers of "Wokeness" have relented, January 18, 2022, https://theupheaval.substack.com/p/no-the-revolution-isnt-over?fbclid=IwAR1qejiu22-Io1wplMtz07ByMhEPe8sKYPsbumba-2r-ZNLRbxWOIfpRpjU&s=r
[170] "Michael Powell on Race, Class, and Free Speech," Persuasion Podcast, November 20, 2021
[171] Rabbi Barry Block, "Social justice should not be controversial," *Times of Israel,* December 4, 2021
[172] "Jewish Americans in 2020," Pew Research Center, May 11, 2021
[173] Greenberg, "Politics of Tikkun Olam," *Sapir*, Spring 2021
[174] Quoted in David Bernstein, "Why We Need a Bigger, Deeper Tikkun Olam," *Jewish Journal*, November 20, 2019
[175] Jonathan Neumann, *To Heal the World?: How the Jewish Left Corrupts Judaism and Endangers Israel,* All Points Books, June 26, 2018
[176] Jonathan Neumann, "Liberal Jews are destroying their own religion," *New York Post,* June 23, 2018
[177] Andrés Spokoiny, "Tikkun Olam: A Defense and a Critique," *eJewish Philanthropy*, October 17, 2018
[178] Quoted in Howard Husock, "Nathan Glazer's Warning: Social policy often does more harm than good, says one of the last of the original neocons," *City Journal*, Summer 2011

[179] "First Step Act: A Team Effort Years In The Making," Statement Floor Statement by Senator Chuck Grassley of Iowa, December 19, 2018

[180] Greenberg, "Politics of Tikkun Olam," Sapir, Spring 2021

[181] "The Delegitimization Challenge: Creating a Political Firewall," Reut, February 14, 2010

[182] Taiyler Simone Mitchell, "The head of the NAACP said the organization is 'reinvigorating' to attract younger members," *Associate Press*, Jan 21, 2022

[183] "Immigration Attitudes and Conspiratorial Thinkers: A Study Issued on the 10th Anniversary of The Associated Press-NORC Center for Public Affairs Research," May 9, 2022

[184] Masood Farivar, "What is the Great Replacement Theory?" *Voice of America*, May 18, 2022

[185] Mounk, *The Great Experiment*, April 19, 2022

[186] Jewish Community Relations Council, https://jewishphilly.org/get-involved/public-affairs-2/

[187] Steven Windmueller, Ph.D., "Rosh Hashanah 5782: Jewish musings on the state of our community," *eJewish Philanthropy*, September 1, 2021

[188] Sophie Bearman, "Meet The Parents Behind An Effort To Recall Three SF School Board Members," *The San Francisco Standard*, March 3, 2021

[189] Ibid.

[190] Erec Smith, "Black People Who Oppose Critical Race Theory Are Being Erased," *Newsweek*, September 7, 2021

[191] Erec Smith, "Free Black Thought: A Manifesto," *Persuasion*, May 5, 2021

ACKNOWLEDGMENTS

When I left my job in the heart of the American Jewish establishment in the Winter of 2021, I had a burning desire to write a book about the growing threat of woke ideology to the Jewish community. I had experienced the dangers firsthand and thought I had a lot to say. But when I put pen to paper I realized that I did not yet have enough experience countering the ascendant dogma to render a coherent argument over multiple chapters. I ended up writing a series of articles instead. One year later, after founding the Jewish Institute for Liberal Values (JILV), now with a rich array of experience under my belt, it all came together.

I am grateful for all the supporters, donors, friends, and family who made possible my pivot into defending the liberal project and opposing a new strain of antisemitism. I've made so many new friends in the endeavor: fellow thought criminals who, like me, couldn't toe the party line even if they tried. I especially thank Daniel Newman, my friend from college, who helped launch the JILV and continues to build the organization brick by brick, and Dr. Brandy Shufutinsky, who does yeoman's work in educating the Jewish community on the dangers of woke ideology and building bridges to new partners. I also thank JILV's Board members, especially our chair, Dr. Pamela Paresky, not only for her early and continued support, but for her articulation of some of the key ideas in the book in her own writing and speaking. I also thank the Nagen Project—especially Richard Gitlin, David Roth, Bobby Casper, and Billy Weinstein—for their vision, partnership, and support.

When I left the comfort of the mainstream Jewish establishment to fight for liberal values and oppose woke ideology, some of my friends and colleagues magically vanished (many others did not). I've since made some truly wonderful new friends in the liberal space, such as Peter Boghossian, Jennifer Richmond, Andrew Gutmann, Zander Keig, Jake Mackey, Greg Thomas, Erec Smith, Wai Wah Chin, George Lee, Paul Rossi, Iona Italia, David Ben Moshe, Monica Osborne, and Jodi Shaw. Thank you all for your support.

My wife Dipika did not hesitate for one second when I traveled into the unknown to build a new organization. She threw her support behind me from the get-go, including taking on the book project. She is the best *chavrutah* partner I could ever ask for and has made the entire book better at every stage, as I read the various sections to her aloud sitting in bed. Even when she was tired, late at night with her eyes closed, pretending to be asleep, she'd suddenly blurt out the perfect edit.

It's truly an honor that Natan Sharansky, the great Soviet refusenik and Jewish leader, wrote the Foreword to this book. Natan exemplifies moral courage: the qualities and actions it takes to overcome a totalizing ideology, not unlike one that he faced down in the Former Soviet Union. I thank him for his continued inspiration.

Michael Pasternak, my close friend since college, told me several months ago that I had enough material to write a book, that I should stop procrastinating, and that it would not take long to get it done. He was right on all counts. When I shared with him my various ideas for a book title, he told me they all stank and—having recently read "Woke Racism" by John McWhorter—insisted that I title the book "Woke Antisemitism." Another good call on his part. Michael makes a few cameos in the book. Another good friend growing up, Michael Golding, contributed by introducing me to all manner of thinkers and writers from a very early age and incessantly debating their ideas with me. We continue this practice until this day. In the Fall of 2021, I participated in an excellent writing workshop put on by the author and podcaster Megan Daum. The workshop participants shared their writing with each other, and I was fortunate to come across that of Rhonda Rockwell, formerly a writing instructor at Harvard, whose riveting story about her father's antisemitism caught my attention. Rhonda edited this book, chapter by chapter. To the degree my prose sparkles, it's all her doing. In lieu of her usual fee, Rhonda asked that I donate money to support the people of Ukraine, which I've happily done. May that besieged nation know peace.

Thanks to my publisher Post Hill Press and Wicked Son books, especially my namesake, David S. Bernstein, for taking on the project. You had me at Wicked Son, my favorite figure at the Passover table.

I thank my parents, Jack and Amira Bernstein, for providing the kind of childhood that gave me material for a book and then some. They were and are always there to cheer me on. And, finally, I thank my kids, Josh, Ari, Maia, and Shaylan for their love and patience. They've each in their own way unknowingly contributed to the writing of this book.

ABOUT THE AUTHOR

Photo by Shmulik Almany

A passionate advocate for the free expression of ideas, David L. Bernstein is the founder of the Jewish Institute for Liberal Values (JILV), which supports viewpoint diversity, counters woke ideology in the Jewish community, and opposes novel forms of antisemitism emerging from woke ideology. Bernstein served as President and CEO of the Jewish Council for Public Affairs, a national umbrella for local Jewish advocacy. He served as Executive Director of The David Project(TDP), which educated and trained American college and high school students in Israel advocacy. He also held senior roles with the American Jewish Committee (AJC), where he began as director of the Washington regional office and served in management roles, overseeing regional offices as well as national and local programming and advocacy. Bernstein has been a leading advocate for Israel's quest for peace and security on the legislative, diplomatic, media, and intergroup relations fronts.